JESUS AS A SOUL-WINNER

Jesus as a Soul-Winner

And Other Evangelistic Messages

By

A. T. ROBERTSON

BAKER BOOK HOUSE
Grand Rapids, Michigan

Printed in the United States of America

To

WILLIAM LOUIS POTEAT, LL.D.,
Professor of Biology and President Emeritus
of Wake Forest College, North Carolina,
the great scientist who first taught
me the elements of Greek.

CONTENTS

I

JESUS AS A SOUL-WINNER

John 4:4-42

THE Gospels constantly picture Jesus as blessing the multitudes by His teaching and healing. He went about doing good, and only good. But in the vivid narrative in John 4:4-42 we catch a glimpse of Jesus winning a soul under the most difficult circumstances. It is not a fancy sketch by a second century writer to glorify Jesus, but a graphic recital of the facts by the Apostle John, who got the story from the woman and from Jesus. With superb skill John shows us the Master in actual contact with an individual soul, precisely the point where so many ministers fail, who may preach eloquent sermons to the crowd. And yet most people who are won to Christ are brought, one at a time, as the result of a personal word. If Christians had the courage and the skill to use their conversation, even with strangers, as a means of leading men to Christ, the Kingdom would spread gloriously. Here we catch Christ in action with a specific case.

1. Though Worn Out from Travel, Jesus Roused Himself at This Opportunity.

The Master was leaving Judæa because His great popularity there had, during the early Judæan ministry, aroused the jealousy and hostility of the Pharisees. They had already inveigled the Baptist into the clutches of Herod Antipas, and now Jesus was making and baptizing more disciples than John was doing. So Jesus turned back to Galilee where His home was, and where His reputation was not yet so great as in Judæa. The direct route north lay through Samaria, and at the close of a day's journey at six P.M. (Roman time, as in all of John's Gospel, there being no longer any Jewish time), Jesus was sitting on the curbstone of Jacob's well at Sychar, a cistern a hundred feet deep, waiting for the disciples to come back from town with food. He was sitting "thus," John says, "wearied from the day's journey." John's Gospel was written to prove the deity of Jesus Christ, yet no Gospel brings out more sharply the human side of the Master's emotions. He was thoroughly tired and was resting, completely relaxed (state of weariness, as the perfect participle shows). But a woman of Samaria comes at the evening hour with her water-pot to draw water, as the peasant women still do in Palestine. She was a stranger to Jesus, and His weariness was excuse enough for Him not to try to win her soul. But Jesus was never too tired to do good, and so He took the initiative Himself. We do not wish to be obtrusive, and so let the golden moment slip by. But Jesus took hold at once with a request.

2. Jesus Asked for a Drink of Water.

He started His interview with the woman on the common basis of interest between them, a drink of water. He was Himself thirsty, and she had come for water. So He said simply, "Give me a drink" (to drink, in the Greek). It was all natural enough for a weary traveller to make such a request, for the woman had her water-pot with her. Water from this famous well was a real need for both Jesus and the woman. Soul-winners make a stupendous blunder by a direct attack on the citadel of the soul, like the overwrought preacher who met a man on the road and blurted out, "Sir, are you prepared to die?" The poor man thought a bandit was holding him up. The poorest way in the world is to apply a rule of thumb out of some handbook, and to put the victim through a catechism. At once the inquirer is put on the defensive and begins to resist. With consummate skill Jesus uses the finest psychological and pedagogic principles by not revealing His purpose at first. But the request of the stranger piqued the woman's curiosity. Instead of granting His courteous request, she had a question of her own to ask.

3. Jesus Rose Above Race and Sex Prejudice.

This is what amazed the woman: "How dost thou, being a Jew, ask a drink from me, being a Samaritan woman?" She was both a woman and a Samaritan.

John adds an explanation (absent in some manuscripts): "For Jews have no dealings with Samaritans." It was an old feud, due primarily to the mixed character of the Samaritan people, Jews left in the land at the Captivity mixing with Gentiles that came in. This antipathy appears in Josephus in connection with the coming of Alexander the Great, who allowed a temple to be built on Mt. Gerizim which was destroyed by John Hyrcanus, who had the Samaritans circumcised. They became Jews nominally, but at heart retained their hatred for their neighbours. When Jesus and the disciples were going through Samaria toward Jerusalem, the Samaritans indignantly refused a welcome for them (Luke 9:52). It is noteworthy that Jesus always speaks kindly to and of Samaritans. It was a Samaritan that had pity on the victim of the robbers, scornfully passed by on the part of priest and Levite. It was the Samaritan alone of the ten lepers who returned and gave thanks to Jesus. When the Pharisees grew angry beyond all bounds at the feast of tabernacles, they said to Jesus: "Say we not well that thou art a Samaritan, and hast a demon?" (John 8:48). They could think of nothing meaner to say. Jesus overcame the race and national prejudice of His day and brushed it aside as nothing. And yet He knew that it existed and that for a while it was a practical barrier to the work of the disciples (Matt. 10:5 f), though Samaria and the limit of the earth came within the horizon of Christ's plan (Acts 1:8).

The work of Philip in Samaria shows that Jesus was understood on this point (Acts 8). Here even the disciples were astonished when they returned and found the Master "talking with a woman" (verse 27), not "talking with the woman," as the King James Version has it. There is no article in the Greek, and the disciples did not know the character of this woman. It was considered improper for a rabbi to be seen talking even with his own wife in public. Will women ever know how much they owe to Jesus? He has made them free indeed, slowly it is true, and not everywhere yet. Paul will catch His spirit, and will claim in Christ freedom from race and national prejudice, class prejudice, sex prejudice (Gal. 3:28; Col. 3:11). The surprising thing is that Jesus calmly rose above all this intense prejudice. Gandhi, Hindu though he is, has been stoned by the high-class Hindus because he championed the cause of the untouchables. We allow far slighter excuses to silence an impulse to win people to Christ.

4. Jesus Turned the Woman's Thoughts to Spiritual Things.

He made a parable of the water, and told her of the water of life: "If thou knewest the gift of God, and who is the one who says to thee, 'Give me to drink,' thou wouldst have asked of him, and he would have given thee living water." She did not understand "the gift of God," as set forth in John 3:16, but she caught at this new kind of water that Jesus claimed to be able to give, "living water." Apparently she thought of spring water, like a gurgling fountain in contrast with the cistern beside which they were, the gift of Jacob. Jesus did not even have a rope to draw water out of this deep well and she marvelled whence this stranger would draw "the living water." "Art thou greater than our father Jacob?" It was a quick retort and showed her interest, though she was still far from grasping the meaning of Jesus. Some people give up in the face of difficulties, but not Jesus.

5. Jesus Persisted in Spite of the Woman's Dulness.

She was still thinking only of literal water for quenching actual thirst. She wanted the water cure. The parable was lost on her. Jesus explains that this "living water" will really quench thirst, for "it will become in him (any one who drinks it) a fountain of water leaping up into eternal life," like a perpetual spring that bursts out of the rocks in a ceaseless flow. Doubtless the woman's eyes sparkled at this glowing picture, and she had a picture of such a fountain in her home, so that she would be spared this tiresome trip once or twice every day to Jacob's well: "Sir, give me this water, that I may not be thirsty and may not keep on coming here to draw." It was a fascinating dream, after the fashion of our modern conveniences for water in our homes. But she had utterly failed to grasp the meaning of Jesus. And Jesus saw her failure, but did not lose patience nor give her up as a hopeless case, as we so often do. He no longer dealt in metaphors nor figures of speech.

6. He Made a Personal Thrust to Reach Her Conscience.

"Go, call thy husband," Jesus says abruptly, but not unkindly. It was a home-thrust, a bolt from the blue. In her surprise and desire to avoid facing this stranger in her real domestic situation, she tried a dodge to evade the issue and said simply: "I have no husband." In that statement she told a half-truth which she hoped would satisfy this strange curiosity about her private life. The talk about the wonderful living water that bubbled up into eternal life was one thing, but prying into her private life was quite another story. So she made an airy reply in the nature of a bluff: "I have no husband." That was true in one sense, for the Greek word for husband (*anēr*) means also man. But the surprise of her life came when this stranger calmly replied: "Well didst thou say, I have no husband; for thou didst have five men, and he whom thou now hast is not thy husband" (in the true sense). This intimate and accurate knowledge of her life on the part of a perfect stranger showed that He was an extraordinary person. She at once admits His insight and pays Him a compliment: "Sir, I perceive that a prophet art thou." Thus only could He know her real life so correctly.

7. Jesus Was Not Thrown Off by the Woman's Desire to Change the Subject.

The turn that she took is an old and a common one. Students try it on the professor when they do not know the lesson. This woman did not care to have a discussion of her living with five men without divorce and remarriage. Her quick wit seized upon the ancient controversy between the Jews and the Samaritans as to the proper place to worship God; whether in the Temple in Jerusalem, or on Mount Gerizim rising above Jacob's well. It was an artful dodge and would have succeeded with some preachers, but not with Jesus. In personal interviews, I have many a time had those under conviction of sin try to turn the talk from their own sins to theological problems which must be settled before surrender to Christ. Jesus does not decline to answer her inquiry, whatever her motive, but He gives her one of the profoundest truths of His teaching, that God is Spirit, and is independent of place and nation, and is to be worshipped in spirit and truth anywhere by any one, whether Jew, Samaritan, or Gentile. But Jesus insisted that salvation is of the Jews, an historical fact that some "German" Christians need to learn today. The answer of Jesus left no room for theological debate, while it completely disposed of the turn taken by the woman. She made one more effort to wave aside any personal responsibility in the matter: "I know that Messias comes, the one called Christ; whenever he comes he will declare to us all things." Meantime, she means, there is no occasion for special concern on the subject. This attitude of indifference, whether real or assumed, has marked the ruin of many a soul.

8. Jesus Told Her His Great Secret.

With sheer simplicity Jesus said to this sinful Samaritan woman: "I am he, the one speaking to thee." There was, beyond a doubt, a mental shock to the woman, not fear but a flash of light upon her soul, that revealed Him as the Living Water of which He had spoken, that "bubbled up into eternal life." The Light and the Life entered into her soul, and now she understood His knowledge of her life. She took Him at His word and was saved. Let us thank God that the way of life is so simple as this, like the trust of a little child, of un untutored woman. The learned Pharisee, Nicodemus, had grave theological difficulties to overcome before he was able to take an open stand for Jesus as the Messiah. Jesus revealed Himself as the Messiah to His disciples at first, and He was so identified by the Baptist. But the word had such powerful political meaning that He ceased till the very end to use the word, for He would be brought into collision with the Pharisees and the Roman authorities. John's Gospel agrees with the Synoptics in showing Christ's restraint on this point. But Jesus told the blessed truth to this woman.

9. Jesus Rejoiced Over the Conversion of This Soul.

The disciples came back at this point with the food from the town, and they were amazed to see the Master talking with a woman, though no one dared express his astonishment. Meanwhile in her new-found joy she left her water-pot and went off to the city, to tell her story to her neighbours who knew her evil life: "Come, see a man who told me all things that I did. Can this one be the Messiah?" She piqued their curiosity by her way of putting it, so that they rushed out of town and went streaming to Jesus. Meanwhile the disciples were puzzled over the lack of appetite in the Master, who said: "I have food to eat of which you do not know." It was the joy of winning a soul, and of doing the Father's will. This is heaven on earth to the soul-winner, to see the light break into the heart and face of a lost sinner. This was Christ's real work. He had won a Samaritan, besides. Dr. R. W. Dale says: "I have seen the sunrise from the top of Helvellyn and the top of the Rigi, and there is something very glorious in it; but to see the light of heaven suddenly strike on man after man in the course of one evening is very much more thrilling."

10. Jesus Caught a Glimpse of the Harvest of the World.

If a Samaritan, and such a one as this sinful woman, can be saved, any one can be. It may have been four months to the harvest, or there may have been a proverb to that effect. It matters little, for Jesus saw the harvest ripe in Samaria, as the people flocked around Him, and all over the world. There is no room, with such a harvest before one, for race prejudice, class prejudice, or any other kind. There is no room in such a harvest for jealousy among preachers or other Christian workers. One sows, another reaps. As Schley said at Santiago, there is glory enough for all. It is pettiness in the pastor or the evangelist to quibble over honour in winning souls to Christ. We need the sower and we need the reaper. We need the preacher and we need the teacher. There is work for the parents and the Sunday-school teachers.

11. The Samaritan Revival the Woman's Reward.

Many believed in Jesus at once because of the saying of the woman. They besought Jesus to spend some days in Sychar, which He gladly did. Then many more believed, and proudly said to the woman: "No longer do we believe because of thy saying; for we ourselves have heard and we know this one is truly the Saviour of the world." The woman was still right, but they had the confirmatory evidence of their own experience. And they call Jesus not the Messiah of the Jews or of the Samaritans, though He was both, but "the Saviour of the world." These Samaritans caught the world mission of Jesus and boldly proclaimed it, apart from national prejudice. This is missions, this is evangelism, this is the gospel for all the world today.

II

CHRIST'S CALL FOR PREACHERS

"And when it was day, he called his disciples; and he chose from them twelve, whom also he named apostles."—LUKE 6:13.

THESE words of Luke refer to the time when Jesus "went out into the mountain to pray; and he continued all night in prayer to God" (ver. 12). Mark (3:14) says that He "appointed twelve that they might be with him." Matthew (9:35–10:5) does not name the twelve apostles till the Master sent them "by two and two" (Mark 6:7), on the third tour of Galilee. These men had been with Jesus for over a year, and now He was moved with compassion for the crowds, because they were distressed and scattered, "as sheep not having a shepherd." It is time for these men to try their hand at preaching and healing. "The harvest truly is plenteous, but the labourers are few. Pray ye therefore the Lord of the harvest, that he send forth labourers into his harvest." They were to pray for workers, and they were to go themselves. One seldom hears a preacher pray for more preachers to enter the harvest. It is a poor church that does not produce preachers, a sign of spiritual vitality. It is interesting to study the words used in the New Testament to describe the kind of men that Jesus calls into the harvest fields. Each word presents a different angle for the picture of the same man and his work.

1. **Learners** *(mathētai).*

We are used to the Latin word "disciple," from *disco,* to learn. That is precisely what the Greek word *mathētēs* means, a learner. Originally the word was used of any and all who took Jesus as Teacher. It was at first a very small group of half a dozen (Andrew and Peter, James and John, Philip and Nathanael), as we see them in the early chapters of John's Gospel (2:11, 12, 22; 4:8, 27, 32), at Bethany beyond Jordan, Cana in Galilee, Capernaum, Jerusalem, Sychar in Samaria. These were simple learners who afterwards went back to their tasks in Galilee. Four of them (Andrew and Simon, James and John) were called to become fishers of men, and left their business to follow Jesus all the time. The term "disciple" came to be applied to all the followers of Jesus, as in John 6:66; Luke 6:13 (our text); and Luke 6:17, "a great multitude of his disciples." In the Acts "the disciples" are those who confess Jesus as the Messiah or the Saviour, a great number in Jerusalem (Acts 6:7). But in the Gospels the word is often used for the twelve men chosen from among the multitude of disciples, "his twelve disciples" (Matt. 10:1). This limited use of the term, for the men chosen after a night of prayer, does not alter the real meaning. They were to be learners. "Take my yoke upon you and learn from me" (Matt. 11:29). This command is given to all who are willing to learn from Jesus, but it concerns preachers in particular. They are expected to have expert knowledge of Jesus and to be able to teach others what they have themselves learned. The preacher who does not keep on learning will die of dry rot. The dead line in the ministry is reached the day that a man stops learning. The true disciple keeps an open mind to God in Christ, to God's Word, and to God's world. He is always growing in grace and in knowledge. Such a preacher is richer and more powerful the older he grows.

2. Workers *(ergatai)*.

The translation "labourers" is a Latin word, but the Greek word is from *ergon* (work). The Anglo-Saxon word "worker" is better. The preacher is to be a worker, not an idler, not a critic. The ripe harvest calls for reapers who are willing and able to put in the scythe and harvest the grain before it is too late. There is never an over-supply of workers in this harvest of the world. There may be too many in a given spot, but there are thousands in every city who are not reached by our organized Christian machinery. This is not a criticism of the churches nor of the preachers, unless they are guilty of neglect. In the first century every Christian was a worker. When the disciples were driven by persecution out of Jerusalem, they scattered the message of the Gospel as they fled. It is necessary to have pastors of churches who are paid salaries, but we need today a new enlistment of the multitude of the disciples as workers, who will carry the story of Jesus to every home in the world. John Wesley and Charles Spurgeon made large use of lay preachers, men who kept their business tasks and on Sunday went into the villages and slums to preach Christ. The city church today grows where its members are like a hive of bees. The workers go out after the honey and fill the hives, not the shirkers or the jerkers. May God hurl forth workers into the harvest, men and women who have learned the truth as it is in Jesus.

3. **Missionaries** *(apostoloi)*.

The Greek word apostle we largely confine to the twelve disciples chosen by Jesus. They did form a special group, to which no one was ever added save Matthias, to take the place of the traitor Judas. Paul was an apostle on a par with the twelve, but not one of the number. So also, Barnabas, Silas, Timothy, James the brother of Jesus, were all apostles in a real sense, as men sent of God. Our word missionary is simply one sent. Jesus Christ is God's Apostle or Missionary to earth (John 17:3; Heb. 3:1). The original meaning of messenger or missionary appears in II Cor. 8:23, where the agents appointed by the churches to help Paul in the collection are called "apostles (messengers), of the churches." John the Baptist is aptly described in John 1:6 as "a man sent from God." So he was, and so are we. God sends us, but not all go when God sends. Some, to be sure, may go whom God did not send. In a true sense, all the workers and learners are sent into the harvest by God. Some, alas, tarry till the eleventh hour. Some pass their responsibility on to the preachers and to the missionaries. The true preacher is a missionary, whether he stays at home or goes to a foreign land. One thing is certain: If all the pastors at home were real missionaries, there would be no lack of support of the work abroad. There are too many hardshells in the pulpit and certainly too many in the pew.

4. **Heralds** *(kērukes)*.

The substantive *kērux* means a herald vested with public authority, who carried the official messages of kings, governors, or military commanders. Paul so conceives of himself as a herald or preacher of Christ (I Tim. 2:7; II Tim. 1:11). He held this to be an honour like being an ambassador *(presbeuō)* for Christ (II Cor. 5:20), equipped with Christ's authority to offer men the terms of reconciliation and peace with God. The verb *kērussō,* to act as herald, to proclaim, is common in the Gospels of the preaching of the Baptist (Matt. 3:1), and of Jesus, who "went about in all the cities and villages teaching in their synagogues and preaching the gospel of the kingdom" (Matt. 9:35). Jesus uses this very word to the apostles: "As ye go, preach" (Matt. 10:7). Hence ministers are called "preachers," even if they preach poorly. It is a noble conception of the minister as the herald of salvation to men, and calls for men of character and force. The true preacher of Christ holds the highest position on earth, as the spokesman of Jesus Christ. Paul proclaimed repentance towards God and faith in the Lord Jesus in public address and in private visits from house to house (Acts 20:20). He was always a preacher and not just while in the pulpit. That was his throne, but he could preach anywhere, whether in a Jewish synagogue, a teacher's classroom, a private home, by the river-side, in a classic courtroom, before Roman governors, facing a mob that clamoured for his life, with a chain on his right hand, in a prison or a palace.

5. **Teachers** *(didaskaloi)*.

Jesus himself is the great Teacher of the ages, and He rejoiced in being considered Teacher and Lord (John 13:13). The word "rabbi" is rendered by *didaskalos* in Greek (John 1:38). Nicodemus recognized Jesus as a teacher come from God (3:10). The publicans called the Baptist "teacher" (Luke 3:12). Paul conceived himself to be "a teacher of the Gentiles" as well as "a herald and apostle." The same man is pictured as teacher who is learner, worker, missionary, apostle. This is an essential aspect of the preacher's task. He must know his message and be able to impart it. Not all men are "apt to teach," though Paul lists this quality in the prerequisites for the preacher. Some indeed are more gifted in teaching than others. Paul mentions "teachers" as a special group of those with the gifts of the Spirit (Eph. 4:11). In the early days in America (Sprague's *Annals of American Ministers*) there would often be two sermons, one the exposition of the text, and the other the exhortation based on it. Now the same man has to do both, and all within a half hour. But the exhortation goes down better if it rests on some solid exposition.

6. **Prophets** *(prophētai)*.

The prophet is one who speaks forth a message, and in particular, a message from God. He is God's spokesman, as Aaron was Moses' prophet (Ex. 7:1). The message of God was by no means always about the future, but more commonly concerning present duty. There was always the sense of urgency. There was a long line of noble prophets in the Old Testament times, which reached its climax in the Baptist, who was more than a prophet. The people took Jesus to be the prophet who was to come into the world (John 6:11), and so He was, though very much more. There were prophets and teachers in the church at Antioch (Acts 13:1-3). The prophet is in touch with God, and has the courage to declare God's will whether men like it or not. Every preacher of Christ today is a prophet, if he is true to his Master and dares to proclaim the whole message of God to his generation. Such courage often resulted in the death of the prophet, who was loyal to his convictions and to his God. But the prophetic note is needed today. The time-serving preacher is a coward, while the prophet is a hero for truth.

7. **Evangelists** *(euaggelistai)*.

In a word, gospelizers, for gospel is *euaggelion.* The gospelizer is one who knows the gospel of God, the good news of salvation, and tells it to the audience or to the individual; who knows how to win men to Christ. The verb *euaggelizomai* is used of the Baptist (Luke 3:18) and of Jesus, "preaching and evangelizing the kingdom of God" (Luke 8:1). Philip is called an evangelist (Acts 21:8), and Paul exhorted Timothy to do the work of an evangelist (II Tim. 4:5). It is a pity to see a preacher who can preach a great sermon and yet is unable to tell a soul how to trust Christ and be saved. The best type of preacher is the pastor-evangelist, who knows how to clinch the sermon with the personal application to the individual. The good fisherman lands his fish. He knows how to draw the net. Some men possess this gift more than others, as Paul noted (I Cor. 12:9; Eph. 4:11). But no preacher should be helpless with one who longs to see Jesus. There is a prejudice against some professional evangelists with tricks of manner and method, but evangelism is the first step in all Christian work. First catch your man for Christ.

8. **Pastors, Shepherds** *(poimenes)*.

Jesus called himself the Good Shepherd (John 10:11). He has the shepherd heart and yearns for the sheep without a shepherd, and for the one lost sheep on the mountainside. In Hebrews 13:20, Jesus is called "the Great Shepherd of the sheep." Peter speaks of Him as "the Shepherd and Bishop of your souls" (I Pet. 2:25), and "the Chief Shepherd" (5:4). By the Sea of Galilee, Jesus said to Peter: "Shepherd my lambs" (John 21:16), "Feed my lambs" (21:15, 17). Paul exhorts the elders (bishops) of Ephesus at Miletus "to shepherd the church of God" (Acts 20:28). And in Ephesians 4:11 he lists shepherds as one of the groups of workers for God along with apostles, prophets, evangelists, teachers. Here again every pastor (Latin for shepherd) is by his very office a shepherd. Some, to be sure, are better shepherds than others. Not long ago, when I preached at a large church, the pastor called attention to an item in the church bulletin stating the fact that two hundred and forty names had been dropped from the roll of over three thousand. Here was not one lost sheep, but a huge flock of two hundred and forty that had wandered away from the fold.

9. Elders *(presbuteroi).*

The word means simply an older man, but it soon came to be applied to officers of a town, like our alderman, and the Jews used it for the rulers of the synagogue and for one form of membership in the Sanhedrin. The earliest use of the word in the New Testament for ministers of Christ is in Acts 11:36, in Jerusalem. They are separate from the apostles (15:2, 22, etc.) and deacons (Phil. 1:1). This use has nothing to do with age, but only with office. There is a natural presumption that one increases in wisdom with age, though it is not always true. Japan used to depend much on the guidance of the Elder Statesmen. Youth has a right to look to age for wisdom. James, the half-brother of Jesus, came to be the leading elder in the church at Jerusalem (Acts 21:18), because of his character and gifts and because the apostles were usually away on preaching tours. Each church in the large cities apparently had several elders, as in Jerusalem (Acts 21:18), Ephesus (20:17), Philippi (Phil. 1:1). This situation probably did not apply to "the church in the house" arrangement, as in the case of Priscilla and Aquila in Rome (Rom. 16:5). Today some ministers insist on using "Elder" before their names instead of Reverend (a non-scriptural term).

10. Bishops *(episcopai)*.

The word means overseer, one who looks over (not overlooks) the concerns of the church of which he is pastor. Peter calls Christ the Bishop of our souls (I Pet. 2:25). The same men are called both elders and bishops in Acts 20:17, 28 and Titus 1:5, 7. The usage in the Epistle of Ignatius (early second century), and common today, of bishop over the elders, does not occur in the New Testament. The apostles did possess leadership over all the churches, but they had no successors in the nature of the case, for personal witnesses of the life and resurrection of Christ came to a natural end (Acts 1:22). There is no rank in the New Testament ministry except that of the apostles. The same men are termed disciples, workers, heralds, teachers, prophets, pastors, elders, bishops. There are diversities of gifts among them, as among the apostles themselves, and so some, like James in Jerusalem, naturally forged ahead into leadership. Paul left Titus in Crete, and Timothy in Ephesus, in charge of the work as superintendents or secretaries of the mission work, a step towards episcopacy, and yet not going beyond the essential New Testament democracy.

11. Ministers *(diakonoi).*

This word *diakonos* occurs technically for deacon in Philippians 1:1 and I Timothy 3:8-13; but it is more frequently applied to preachers as ministers of Christ. In itself it is simply any one who serves with diligence (raises a dust by hastening), whether his master be householder (John 2:5, 9), king (Matt. 22:13), or God (Rom. 13:4). Paul rejoiced to call himself a minister of the gospel (Col. 1:23), and of the church (1:25), and in particular of Christ (II Cor. 11:23). Jesus used the verb (*diakoneō,* to serve) of Himself, as expressing His conception of His own mission (Matt. 20:28). "Whoever wishes to become great among you shall be your servant" (*diakonos,* Matt. 20:26). That is Christ's idea of true greatness, great service to others in Christ's name. The greatest preacher in Christ's view may be one of whom we have never heard, one who served best in the place where he laboured. There are other words somewhat parallel to *diakonos* like *hupēretēs* (under-rower), used of Mark (Acts 13:5), and *halieus* (fisherman), used of the four by the Sea of Galilee, who were to become fishers of men (Mark 1:17).

12. Witnesses *(martures)*.

Our English word "martyr" is this very word, one who witnesses with his death, like Stephen. Jesus expressly charged the disciples to wait for the promise of the Father, the coming of the Holy Spirit in power (Luke 24:48 f.; Acts 1:4). Then, "ye shall be my witnesses." Now a witness can only testify in court what he knows himself, not what he has heard someone else say. It would have been a tragedy if the disciples, before they were clothed with power from on high, had gone forth to take the world for Christ. The Holy Spirit enabled them to understand the things of Christ. They already had faith and hope, but now they gained insight and power. Hence Peter boldly said: "This Jesus did God raise from the dead, of whom we all are witnesses" (Acts 2:32). When arraigned before the Sanhedrin, Peter and John bravely defied this Jewish court: "We are not able not to go on speaking the things which we saw and heard" (4:20). Such witnesses are irresistible. It is pitiful to hear a preacher talk about Christ without personal knowledge of Him as Saviour. Such a preacher is powerless, however gifted he may be, and whatever degrees he may have. Instance Spurgeon and Moody, as men who were filled with the power of the Holy Spirit. Thomas Chalmers says that he preached twelve years before he was converted. After that he became Scotland's greatest preacher of Christ.

III

THE CRUCIFIED LIFE

"I have been crucified with Christ; and no longer do I live, but Christ lives in me: and what life I now live in the flesh, I live by faith in the Son of God, who loved me and gave himself for me."—GALATIANS 2:20.

THIS is one of Paul's profound mystical sayings that challenge one, and fascinate one with the depth of their meaning. Paul was one of the most intellectual of men, and yet he was a mystic in the truest sense of that term. He was not carried away by the superficial claims and language of the mystery-religions of the time, like Mithraism, but he never doubted the reality of his own union with Christ. The heart of Christ's work was the Cross, and Paul found contact with Christ in that supreme experience. Paul considered himself a typical sinner, "that in me as chief might Christ Jesus set forth his entire long-suffering for an ensample to those who were going to believe on him unto life eternal" (I Tim. 1:16). So then, since this chief of sinners became the chief of saints, we may study his own relation to the Cross of Christ with profit to all other sinners saved by grace.

1. Christ Crucified for Paul.

The Son of God loved me and gave Himself for me. So Paul says in our text, and so he felt always. The wonder of God's love is shown precisely in this, that "while we were yet sinners, Christ died for us" (Rom. 5:8). This is God's own plan of redemption in Christ Jesus, as the propitiation for our sins (Rom. 3:25), that God may be just and justify the one with faith in Jesus Christ as Saviour. There are many theories of the atoning death of Christ, with an element of truth in most of them, but all put together they fall short of explaining the sublime fact that when we were under the curse of the law Jesus became a curse over us (in our stead), and brought us out from under that curse (Gal. 3:10-13), so that we go free, we who trust Christ for what He has done for us. In a sense beyond our grasping, it is true that "the one who did not know sin he (God) made to be sin for us" (II Cor. 5:21). This supreme fact is the bedrock of Paul's theology, the death of Christ for the sinner, that the sinner may live. So then God has forgiven all our transgressions because of what Christ has done, if we trust Him as Saviour. He has rubbed out the bond that was against us, has cancelled the debt, and has nailed it to the Cross of Christ (Col. 2:13 f). This is the gospel that Paul preached, that Christ died for our sins, was buried, and has been raised on the third day (I Cor. 15:3 f). This is Paul's gospel of grace that he preached everywhere to all classes of men. He was not ashamed of this gospel in Athens or in Rome, for it and it alone is the power of God unto salvation to every one who believes in Jesus Christ. Without the Cross, Paul had no gospel. And there is no salvation in Greek philosophy or Jewish law, "for all sinned and fall short of the glory of God" (Rom. 3:23). Left to himself, Paul with all his pride of race and pious performances (Phil. 3:4-7) was a wretched man with the corpse of his sinful self clinging to him (Rom. 7:24). But he was more than conqueror in Christ who loved him.

2. Paul Crucified with Christ.

Jesus himself had spoken of the union of the believer with Him, like that of the branches with the vine, deriving life from the vine and bearing fruit because of that life-giving union (John 15:1-6). Paul felt the truth of Christ's wonderful image to the full. He died to the law as a means of salvation (Gal. 2:19); he died with Christ from the elements of the world as a means of grace (Col. 2:20); he died to sin and pictured that death and the new walk with Christ, by baptism: "We were buried with him by baptism unto death: that like as Christ was raised up from the dead by the glory of the Father, even so we also should walk in newness of life" (Rom. 6:4). Baptism to Paul symbolized the death, burial, and resurrection of Jesus, Paul's own death to sin and resurrection to a new life, and the resurrection of the body after death. If we died with Christ, we are also raised together with

Christ (Col. 2:20; 3:1). Paul does not think of baptism as the means by which this mystic union is obtained, but as the beautiful picture of the inner experience of the death to sin, and of the new life in Christ already secured. *Noblesse oblige.* Baptism is like the soldier's uniform, the *sacramentum,* the sign of the oath of fealty. The baptized man should lead the baptized life of cleanness and of loyalty. He wears the badge wherever he goes, and should never disgrace the uniform which he wears. He has been buried with Christ. He has been raised with Christ. But baptism is merely the outward sign of the inward experience of one who has been crucified with Christ. When Jesus was nailed to the Cross, in a mystical and yet true sense Paul was nailed there also. Paul's sins helped nail Christ to the Cross. Christ hung on the Cross for Paul, and Paul hung on the Cross with Christ. Paul felt the call to go all the way with Christ to the Cross. Not that there is any virtue in our own sufferings, as the Roman Catholics argue. We do not remove our own sins by persecution of the flesh. But in a real sense we go out with Christ to the Cross and take our stand with Him there, without being ashamed of Him or of His Cross. We go out to Christ outside the camp, bearing His reproach (Heb. 13:13).

3. Christ Living in Paul.

Paul is so identified with Christ that "no longer do I live, but Christ is living in me." The old man of sin has died, and the new man in Christ has taken possession of Paul, the whole of Paul, not just certain compartments. There are no secret chambers in Paul's life to which Christ is not welcome. He has given to Jesus all the keys of his life. This complete surrender of Paul's will to that of Christ has cost him a struggle. He has carried on a fight with his own body to win this victory (I Cor. 9:27). He has had to keep with him the consciousness of the dying of Jesus for him, that the life of Jesus may be manifested in his own body (II Cor. 4:10). There has been in a mystical sense the transfusion of the life-blood of Jesus into Paul's body, that he may live the life that is in Christ Jesus. We must not misunderstand Paul's use of such mystical language of union with Christ. He has no idea of loss of personality or of responsibility, but he means that he has put Christ in control of his own will to such an extent that he can truthfully say: "Christ lives in me." He lives therefore a Christ-filled life. What a glory it would be if all nominal Christians could say that! Gone would be selfishness, love of sin, lives of sin. What a change would come in the church life and the church work. Deficits and debts would no longer exist. Men would indeed take knowledge of us that we had been with Jesus, that Jesus was reproducing Himself in us, that we were in reality the children of God, with some of the likeness of our Elder Brother even here on earth. If we are to be like Him in heaven, the picture ought to be recognizable even here.

4. Paul Carrying His Own Cross After Christ.

Paul knew the teaching of Jesus about taking up one's own cross and following the Master. "And I, in my turn, fill up the remainder of the tribulations of the Christ in my flesh in behalf of his body, which is the church" (Col. 1:24). Jesus met His own Cross bravely, even with foreboding and shrinking, and yet with a certain eagnerness, at times, to have His baptism of blood (Luke 12:50). He "for the joy placed before him endured the cross, despising the shame" (Heb. 12:2), and the Master calls us all to follow His example. So Paul took his turn and his share of suffering for Christ with God's people. Each one of us has his own load to carry. One has only to read Paul's graphic account of his own experiences in the ministry, to see how fully he bore his share of the crosses of life: "persecuted on every side, but not straitened; at a loss, but not utterly lost; pursued, but not left behind; cast down, but not perishing" (II Cor. 4:8 f). Once more hear Paul: "In toils more abundantly, in prisons more frequently, in stripes superabundantly, in deaths often; by the Jews five times did I receive forty stripes save one; thrice was I beaten with rods, once only was I stoned, thrice did I experience shipwreck, a night and a day did I spend in the deep; in journeys often, in perils of rivers, in perils of robbers, in perils from my own race, in perils from Gentiles, in perils in the city, in perils in the wilderness, in perils in the sea, in perils among false brethren, in toil and travail, in watchings often, in hunger and thirst, in fastings often, in cold and nakedness" (II Cor. 11:23-27).

Surely, no servant of Christ, not even Judson in Burmah or Livingstone in Africa, can match this catalogue. But this is not all, for he carried about with him that stake in the flesh, a messenger of Satan to buffet him, to keep him from being overexalted (II Cor. 12:7). The only help he received when he cried out to the Lord was: "My grace is sufficient for thee; for my power is made perfect in weakness." Once the Galatians welcomed Paul as an angel of God, and would have dug out their eyes for him, and then they came to count him as nothing, and to spit out at him in disgust. For my part, I am glad we do not know what was Paul's stake in the flesh. Each of us can find comfort in enduring the crosses in his own life. Each of us can claim Christ's promise of grace sufficient to bear them for Christ's sake. Christ has made the Cross the symbol of glory and of triumph for all time. There is no virtue in wearing a cross as a crucifix or charm, an amulet to ward off evil. But I do like to see a cross on every church, Protestant as well as Catholic. This symbol is not the monopoly of the Roman Catholics.

5. Paul's Glory in the Cross of Christ.

Jesus felt to the utmost the agony and shame of the Cross as He died for the sin of the world. And yet He went on to the Cross and held Himself to it by the

Father's help, in spite of the momentary outcry in Gethsemane. Paul felt the sharp recoil of the cultured Greeks from the Cross as foolishness, and of the Pharisaic Jews as a stumbling-block. The idea of a condemned and crucified criminal, as the Messiah of Jewish hope, was repugnant to all the rabbis. And yet Paul, who once shared the attitude of the Pharisees, came to know nothing among the Corinthians, "save Jesus Christ and this one crucified" (I Cor. 2:2). Already some of the Judaizing Christians were belittling the Cross (Gal. 6:12), to make a fair show in the flesh, just as some preachers today are ashamed of the Cross of Christ and ignore it for a purely social message, or even ridicule it, and yet call themselves ministers of Christ. Let all such men hear Paul: "May it not happen to me to glory except in the cross of our Lord Jesus Christ, by whom the world stands crucified to me and I to the world" (Gal. 6:14).

Christ without the Cross would have been a mere example without redemptive power. Christ glorified the Cross, and Paul glories in the Cross of Christ as the sole ground for exaltation. With Paul the Cross involves the Incarnation and the Resurrection. The mere act of dying could not save men. But this is the Son of God, who left His estate with the Father and humbled Himself to man's estate as the Son of Man; who went all the way to death, even the very death of the Cross (the most shameful of all deaths). But the Father, because of this voluntary humiliation, lifted

Jesus Christ to a higher exaltation. In heaven He is now the Risen Lord Jesus Christ, with both His deity and His humanity. But for the Cross, Jesus could not be our Saviour and Redeemer. And Paul is linked in his life with the Crucified and Risen Lord. So are we all, if we have surrendered our hearts to Jesus Christ. He is our Head, and we are members of His glorious Body. That is dignity enough for any one.

IV

NEHEMIAH, THE BUILDER

"So we built the wall. . . . I am doing a great work, so that I cannot come down."—NEHEMIAH 4:6; 6:3.

THERE are few examples in the Bible or in human history more stimulating than that of Nehemiah, as he rebuilt the wall of Jerusalem under staggering difficulties. Millions of workers for God in all the ages have had to face like difficulties in doing the Lord's work. The preeminent New Testament example is Paul; but Nehemiah went up against a single definite task, and it is positively amazing what hindrances, drawbacks, oppositions he had to overcome, difficulties that would have defeated a weaker nature with less faith in God and less courage of heart. Every pastor, teacher, and church worker will be helped by studying Nehemiah. It was a voluntary task and he could have let it alone.

1. Difficulties in Starting the Work.

(a) *The Greatness and Remoteness of the Task.* Nehemiah was the cupbearer of Artaxerxes, the king in Shushan, when he heard of the sad state of the remnant of Jews left in Jerusalem and how the wall of

Jerusalem was broken down and the gates burned with fire. He could have excused himself, since he was not responsible for it and he was so far away. He was not to blame for this utter ruin, though to the Lord he confesses "the sins of the children of Israel, which we have sinned against thee. Yea, I and my father's house have sinned" (Neh. 1:6). He did not evade his share of the sins of his people. Today we Christians too often absolve ourselves from responsibility for mission work away from our church, our town, our state, our country. We sometimes even confine our responsibility to our own family, and do not always assume that. Nehemiah went to the Lord in prayer and made the situation in Jerusalem his own problem, just as Carey did for India, Judson for Burmah, and Livingstone for Africa. Nehemiah first went to the Lord with his problem to get the power of the Lord.

(b) *Getting the King's Consent.* That he succeeded in doing, difficult as it seemed. His sad countenance interested the king, though Nehemiah "was very sore afraid" (2:2). He told the story of his grief over Jerusalem to the king and queen and won permission to go and obtained letters and a guard to help him on his way. So he came to Jerusalem safely.

(c) *But Confronted by the Hostility of Sanballat and Tobiah.* "But when Sanballat the Horonite, and Tobiah, the Ammonite, heard of it, it grieved them exceedingly, for that there was come a man to seek the welfare of the children of Israel" (2:10). These enemies of the remnant of the Jews in Jerusalem were determined to prevent, if possible, any advance movement that would help the cause of the Jews in the city. Hence Nehemiah had to go warily about his task. So he made a midnight tour of the walls of the city with a handful of faithful men, that he might get the precise facts by first-hand knowledge. Then he called a meeting of the leading Jews and "told them of the hand of my God which was good upon me; as also of the king's words that he had spoken unto me" (2:18), and proposed that they build again the walls of Jerusalem. The leaders said: "Let us rise up and build." But Sanballat and Tobiah "laughed us to scorn and despised us, and said, What is this thing that ye do? Will ye rebel against the king?" That was shrewd, but it did not stop Nehemiah, who replied: "The God of heaven, he will prosper us; therefore we his servants will arise and build: but ye have no portion, nor right, nor memorial, in Jerusalem" (2:20). Sanballat and Tobiah were rank outsiders, and must stand aside. Their scorn and ridicule will not prevent the starting of the enterprise.

(d) *Getting the People to Work.* This is always a problem. Nehemiah devotes a whole chapter (3) to telling how he divided the work among the various clans and classes of the Jews left in Jerusalem. It was all skilfully done. In a number of instances a man repaired the wall "over against his house" (3:10, 23,

28, 29). That was a wise arrangement—each man entrusted with the part of the wall that protected him. In one case, that of Shallum, "he and his daughters" did it (3:12). One example, that of the Tekoites, is mentioned, "but their nobles put not their necks to the work of their Lord" (3:5). These "nobles" were too nice for such manual labour! There are always church members like that, who are too delicate and proper for the details of work in church. So the work got under way. There were some to say that it could not be done.

2. Difficulties in Carrying on the Work.

(a) *Sanballat and Tobiah Tried Mockery.* Sanballat "mocked the Jews before his brethren and the army of Samaria, and said, What do these feeble Jews? will they fortify themselves? will they sacrifice? will they make an end in a day? will they revive the stones out of the heaps of rubbish, seeing they are burned?" (4:2). He felt quite superior in his scorn, precisely as many of the scoffers of Christianity have done through the ages. The very house in Paris where Voltaire wrote his diatribes against Christianity is now a Bible house. Nehemiah did "revive" the very stones out of the rubbish piles and rebuilt the wall. Ezekiel saw in vision the dry bones leap with life again. Many a pastor has seen a dead or dying church wake up to life. The Spirit of God continues to work revivals of men, dead in trespasses and sins, to newness of life in Christ Jesus. Tobiah took up the sneer and said:

"Even that which they build, if a fox go up, he shall break down their stone wall" (4:3). Such ridicule was hard to stand and go on with the work, but Nehemiah and the workers turned to the Lord in prayer and laboured on. "So we built the wall," in spite of the sneers of Sanballat and Tobiah who picked flaws in the work as it went on. The Church has always had critics, and always will, who stand off and point out defects in the churches. Magazine writers and novelists are continually preaching the funeral of the churches, despite the fact that the number of church members in the United States, in proportion to population, is far in excess of any preceding period of our history. A hundred years ago they were proclaiming the death of Christianity, as has been done periodically every century. This wall went up, "for the people had a mind to work." That is what matters. Nothing can stop the work of God when that is true.

(b) *Sanballat and Tobiah Organized a Conspiracy.* They saw that more than ridicule was needed, for the work of repairing the walls went forward and the breaches were being stopped. Sanballat and Tobiah got together the Arabians, the Ammonites, and the Ashdodites, the disgruntled elements, of whom there are always a plenty. "Then they were very wroth; and they conspired all of them together to come and fight against Jerusalem, and to cause confusion therein" (4:8). Judah at once gave in to this pressure and said: "The strength of the bearers of burdens is decayed, and there is much rubbish; so that we are not able to build the wall" (4:10). Thus a breach was made in the ranks of Nehemiah's men. The adversaries were gleeful and planned a secret attack to "slay them, and cause the work to cease." "They shall not know, neither see." But Nehemiah prayed to God and armed the people and the workers, and said: "Be not ye afraid of them: remember the Lord, which is great and terrible, and fight for your brethren, your sons, and your daughters, your wives, and your houses" (4:14). Nehemiah thus flung himself into the breach and saved the day. A crisis tries men's souls and tests character like a fire.

(c) *Working on in Apprehension.* Half the people worked, while the others held their weapons ready for the attack. Then even the workers, every one, held a weapon in one hand and builded with the other, or used his trowel with sword girded by his side. So they worked each day till the stars appeared and the wall grew. Finally, "none of us put off our clothes, every one went with his weapon to the water." There were watchers at exposed places and trumpeters were ready to call, if they had to meet an attack. "Our God shall fight for us," Nehemiah said. They worked on and were also ready to fight. They learned how to work and fight off the oppressors at the same time. Meanwhile the walls kept on going up all round the city.

(d) *Finally there Came an Uprising among the*

Workers Themselves. Like Bunyan's "Fainthearted," some groups exploded and caused a strike. "We, our sons and our daughters, are many: let us get corn that we may eat and live" (5:2). Nehemiah now faced a financial crisis, a period of depression. "We are mortgaging our fields, and our vineyards, and our houses: let us get corn because of the dearth." Famine had caught them and some were victims of usurers or money sharks: "We have borrowed money for the king's tribute upon our fields and our vineyards" (5:4). Their sons and daughters were on the verge of slavery for debt. There was danger of revolt. Nehemiah saw the peril, and boldly faced the men of means and said: "Ye exact usury, every one of his brother." He held an assembly against the loan sharks, and demanded the return to the people of their lands and part of their money, oil, and corn. The usurers surrendered to this demand, and Nehemiah put them on oath and dramatically shook out his lap as a sign of what God would do to any one who was not true to his oath on this point. So the financial crisis was passed and the work went on, for the people rallied again with thanksgiving and praise. "I continued in the work of this wall, neither bought we any land" (5:16). Nehemiah got no personal profit out of the success of the cause. The work went on, all making sacrifices for the common cause.

3. Difficulties in Completing the Task.

(a) *Sanballat and Tobiah now Proposed a Con-*

ference. When Sanballat, Tobiah, and Geshem the Arabian heard that Nehemiah had built the wall with no breaches left, though the doors in the gates were not yet set, they sent word to Nehemiah: "Come, let us meet together in one of the villages in the plain of Ono" (6:2). "They thought to do me mischief," Nehemiah felt, and would not be caught in such a trap. When the enemies of Christ cannot stop the progress of Christianity, they want a conference and a compromise. But Nehemiah brushed them aside with this message: "I am doing a great work, so that I cannot come down: why should the work cease, whilst I leave it, and come down to you?" That is the answer of a hero. Sanballat persisted and four times begged for a conference to talk matters over, just as the devil tempted Jesus three times in succession. But Sanballat failed, as Satan did with Christ. The work went on.

(b) *Then Sanballat Tried to Frighten Nehemiah.* He sent an open letter to Nehemiah with the charge that there was a widespread rumour among the nations, according to Geshem, that Nehemiah was going to rebel against Artaxerxes and be king of Palestine, and that he already had prophets proclaiming that there is a king in Judah (6:5-7). In such a crisis Nehemiah needed help, else this rumour would be sent to the king by Sanballat. "Come now, therefore, and let us take counsel together." It was a shrewd trick, designed to make Nehemiah afraid. It did not succeed, for Nehemiah prayed: "O God, strengthen thou my hands." He sent word to Sanballat that he had made up this lie out of whole cloth: "There are no such things as thou sayest, but thou feignest them out of thine own heart." By raising such a slander Sanballat had hoped to paralyze Nehemiah and his workers: "Their hands shall be weakened from the work, that it be not done." Sanballat had raised an imaginary difficulty to cripple the work. But Nehemiah was a leader with insight, and with courage and faith. He was as shrewd as Sanballat, with character and conviction in addition. A fainthearted or a stupid leader would have been an easy prey for Sanballat's scheme. Sanballat, under the guise of friendship to save him from the king's rage, was stabbing him in the back.

(c) *Nehemiah almost Caught in Another Trap of Sanballat's.* Shemaiah was a tool of Sanballat, and Nehemiah did not know it. He was a spy, and posed as a friend of Nehemiah when he innocently went to see him. Shemaiah enlarged upon the plots against Nehemiah's life and proposed that they go into the house of God and "shut the doors of the temple: for they will come to slay thee; yea, in the night will they come to slay thee" (6:10). It sounded pious and sensible enough, but Nehemiah disliked the idea of fleeing from his enemies as a fugitive. It would look like cowardice and distrust of God. So he replied to Shemaiah: "Should such a man as I flee? and who is there, that, being such as I, would go into the temple to save his life? I will not go in." It was a narrow escape and the scheme had been skilfully planned by Sanballat, but just in time Nehemiah saw through it: "And I discerned, and, lo, God had not sent him: but he pronounced this prophecy against me: and Tobiah and Sanballat had hired him. For this cause was he hired, that I should be afraid, and do so, and sin, and that they might reproach me" (6:10-12). Shemaiah posed as a prophet of God, when in reality he was a hireling of Sanballat and Tobiah, who stopped at nothing to ruin Nehemiah. Alas, that a man will wear the livery of heaven in which to serve the devil. But Paul found that Satan posed as an angel of light. Nehemiah knew that for him to flee to the temple for refuge would give colour to the slander that he was a rebel king. "Walk into my parlour," said the spider to the fly. But this "fly" refused to walk in. If Nehemiah had fled to the temple, Sanballat would have posed as the champion of Artaxerxes against the rebel.

(d) *The Prophetess Noadiah Lent a Hand.* Nehemiah prayed to God: "Remember, O my God, Tobiah and Sanballat according to these their works, and also the prophetess Noadiah, and the rest of the prophets, that would have put me in fear" (6:14). Shemaiah was not the only "prophet" who, "for hire," tried to put Nehemiah in fear. But Noadiah was also a woman, "a female of the species more deadly than the male." This is the only mention of this woman, who passed as a prophetess of God and sold her services to the enemies of God in Jerusalem. The church in Thyatira had a Jezebel in the membership, who played havoc in the church as only an evil woman can. Do not overlook Noadiah when you think of the obstacles in the path of Nehemiah. Many a pastor has had to fight on against propaganda by such a woman. But even the prophetess Noadiah failed to frighten Nehemiah, who stood his ground with superb courage and pushed on the work.

(e) *Last of All Came Treachery Among Some of the Nobles of Judah.* They had been the first to quit working (4:10). Now they are indignant that Nehemiah has succeeded without their help and against their advice. Some of "the nobles" of the Tekoites had refused at the start to work (3:5). So these disgruntled elements wrote letters to Tobiah and he wrote to them (6:17). This put new heart in Tobiah, who once more "sent letters to put me in fear" (6:19). But it was too late. Nehemiah set up the doors and the work was done. Even the enemies "perceived that this work was wrought of our God." There was a proper dedication service when "all the people gathered themselves together as one man into the broad place that was before the water gate; and they spake unto Ezra the scribe to bring the book of the law of Moses, which the Lord had commanded to Israel" (8:1). It was a great and solemn occasion as the people listened to Ezra, while he read the law in the

Hebrew and "gave the sense" in the Aramaic, so that they understood the reading (8:7). Suppose Nehemiah had faltered in his task and his trust. Sanballat and Tobiah and Noadiah would have triumphed and the forces of disorder would have ruled in Jerusalem. Nehemiah was a religious statesman with vision, with faith, and with power.

V

ASAPH'S RECOVERY FROM PESSIMISM

"Truly God is good to Israel, even to such as are of a clean heart. But as for me, my feet were almost gone; my steps had well nigh slipped."—PSALM 73:1, 2.

ASAPH starts up abruptly, as if from a brooding reverie by the fire over the problems of Providence and life. Things had looked dark to him, and he had nearly gone over the cliff of doubt and despair. Now he sees that after all God is good to Israel, little as he once thought it. He appeals to the goodness of God to his people, as giving the rainbow of hope to the black cloud of despondency that had hovered over him. It has been pointed out that in like case, Job appealed to the omniscience of God as a sure support (Job 24:1), Jeremiah to the justice of God (Jer. 12:1), and Habakkuk to the holiness of God (Hab. 1:15). There is truth in each point of view. Matthew Henry has a wonderful analysis of this great experimental Psalm: How the Psalmist Got into Temptation (verses 2–16); How He Got Out of Temptation (verses 17–20); How He Got Past His Temptation (verses 21–28). The whole Psalm is an exposition of verse

1: "Surely God is good to Israel." This is the conclusion stated at the start, as if illustrated in his own case, which can be helpful to all of us.

1. The Psalmist's Absence from the Sanctuary Gave Him a Wrong View of Life.

He grew envious of the wicked, and was unable to understand God's apparent blessing upon them to the neglect of the pious. Several reasons for his envy appear.

(a) *The Temporal Prosperity of the Wicked.* "I was envious at the arrogant, when I saw the prosperity of the wicked. . . . Their eyes stand out with fatness: they have more than heart could wish." The Jews had a theory that temporal prosperity was a mark of the divine favour, but here the very reverse seemed true. "The waters of a full cup are wrung out to them." This is an old story of one who becomes sour in spirit, when he sees wickedness flourishing in high places and the godly victims of misfortune. This is a perpetual riddle to the pious churchgoer who sees the Sunday golfer prosper, while he, who goes regularly to church, laments his poverty. "Being always at ease, they increase in riches. . . . When I thought how I might know this, it was too painful for me."

(b) *The Wicked Seem Free from Trouble.* "There are no bonds (pangs) in their death, but their strength is firm. They are not in trouble as other men; neither are they plagued like other men." This, to be sure, was a short and partial view, but it was one of the reasons that made Asaph hesitate on the brink with slippery feet. It looked as if God had turned over Asaph and other saints to Satan, to buffet and torment, as He did Job. In times of depression the poor and the honest pay their taxes, while some of the rich shrewdly evade their millions of income tax by dodges and legal subterfuges. At times it looks as if a premium is placed on rascality and dishonesty. The cloud was growing blacker for Asaph all the time.

(c) *The Wicked Show Insolence Towards Others.* "Pride is as a chain about their neck; violence covereth them as a garment." It is familiar enough: those in power "scoff, and in wickedness utter oppression." Through the long ages God's people have suffered persecution from rulers in State and even in Church. "They speak loftily. They have set their mouth in the heavens, and their tongue walketh through the earth." In our own time we have had the President of the United States defy the money-changers, who have robbed the people and violated the laws of the land. Brazenly corrupt, these people oppress the poor, defraud banks, flee the country and escape punishment. Often public men are not expected to be honest. Graft and bribery flourish in the seats of government.

(d) *They Talk Against God.* "They say, How doth God know? And is there knowledge in the

Most High?" They laugh and jeer at things holy and sacred, just as in the movies and over the radio today ridicule is heaped upon purity, honesty, and reverence, as old-fashioned and "back-woodsy." The preacher and the Church are held up to scorn, and God is relegated to the realm of superstition. Yet today such philosophy is out of date, and shows calm ignorance of twentieth century thought; for Eddington makes a plea for the spiritual as superior to the material, just as Jesus did. The Psalmist tottered in his reason, as he sought to solve all this doubt by himself. "When I thought how I might know this, it was too painful for me." His feet were almost gone, his steps had well-nigh slipped.

2. Return to the Sanctuary Gave Asaph the True Angle of Vision.

"Until I went into the sanctuary of God," he says, "and considered their latter end." This was, and is, the way out of doubt and despair. Asaph had had a close call, and paid dearly for his long absence from the public worship of God. Many of us have had narrow turns in our lives. I recall one on a crooked and steep mountain road, fortunately before the days of the automobile, when a sudden flash of lightning revealed a sharp curve and a yawning chasm before us. Two things brought Asaph back to his senses.

(a) *He Was Back in the Sanctuary at Last.* Perhaps with cynicism still and a good deal of scepticism. Someone induced him to come back to church. He had lost interest in worship and had no taste for sermons, and probably had no hope of any good from his return to the house of God. But, at any rate, it would do him no harm, and he was willing to risk it once more. "I was glad when they said unto me, Let us go into the house of the Lord," said another Psalmist (Psa. 122:1). Here is the secret for the man with doubts and troubles. Come back to the house of God and seek the Lord in the appointed place of worship by His people. God can be worshipped anywhere, on Mount Gerizim, in Jerusalem, wherever a soul is, who lifts up his thoughts to Him. But God reveals Himself in a special manner to those who seek His face in the house of worship. "Thy way, O God, is in the sanctuary" (Psa. 77:13). Oh, tried and tempted man, come back to God and go not to the camp of the atheists, the anarchists, without God and without hope in the world. "Draw nigh to God, and he will draw nigh to thee" (Jas. 4:8).

In the winter of 1888, D. L. Moody held a month's meetings in Louisville in a tabernacle, where the old Norton Hall of the Southern Baptist Theological Seminary was afterwards erected. It was my last year as a student, and one night I went into the after-meeting in the church next door. I saw a man sitting apart under one end of the gallery. I sat down by him and led him to talk about himself. He said that he was a steamboat captain, on his way from Huntington, West Virginia, to New Orleans. He had not been to church for twenty years. His boat had stopped at Louisville on business. That evening, as he walked out Fourth Avenue to go to a theatre, he saw the advertisement of the Moody and Sankey meetings. He had heard of Sankey, and was fond of music; so he strolled out to the Tabernacle to hear Sankey sing and was willing to put up with Moody's preaching. He did hear Sankey sing "The Ninety and Nine," but he also heard Moody preach, and now he was here in the inquiry room under deep conviction of sin. I had him kneel down and pray aloud for forgiveness. Before he rose from his knees he murmured: "I am so glad that I came here tonight. I must write to my wife tonight about finding God." So he did write his wife in Huntington. He had found God and eternal life by coming back to the sanctuary. Mel Trotter tells the story on himself, that he was on his way to commit suicide in Lake Michigan, when he was induced to step inside the Pacific Garden Mission, where he was saved. Thousands upon thousands can give like witness to finding God in the sanctuary.

(b) *Then He Saw the End of the Wicked.* He had wholly overlooked this aspect of the matter, and had regarded the temporary prosperity of the wicked as permanent. He had not thought of that. He had taken a short and contracted view. Now Asaph sees that the wicked are "in slippery places," just as he had been when filled with doubts. But their prosperity was short, and their destruction sure. "There is a way that seemeth right unto a man; but the end thereof are the ways of death" (Prov. 14:12). "How are they become a desolation?" The collapse is sudden and sure. Asaph is as one awaking out of a dream. It had seemed that God was asleep and did not care. It is the rich man and Lazarus—Lazarus the beggar at the rich man's gate, but now in the life beyond, the rich man is in torment and Lazarus in Abraham's bosom. Wrongs in this life will be corrected on the other side. It is the duty of the Christian capitalist to correct them here and now. There would be no problem of labour and capital if employer and employee met in God's house and acted squarely with each other. Not all the wrongs of life can be corrected here, though many can be. The tares are so mixed in the wheat-field by the evil one, that complete separation can only come at the final harvest. But Lowell is right:

"Truth forever on the scaffold, wrong forever on the throne,—
Yet that scaffold sways the future, and behind the dim unknown,
Standeth God within the shadows, keeping watch above His own."

3. And Good Now Came to Asaph.

(a) *He was Humbled before God.* That came first. "My heart was grieved, and I was pricked in my reins;

so foolish was I and ignorant; I was as a beast before thee." He should not have been envious of the wicked and resentful towards God. Pride ruled in his heart during his absence from the sanctuary. Now he sees his folly and his ignorance. With a broken heart he sees his own picture in its true outline. You cannot teach a proud heart anything. God resists the proud, but gives grace to the humble. God's hand is often hidden in our lives and we see the good in the end. He has a way of overruling even evil for our good. The child little understands his father's plans of love for him and may rebel against the discipline necessary to teach him the ways of righteousness. It was in his prison days that O. Henry learned to write his marvellous short stories. Paul made his prisons gateways to power and to service.

(b) *Asaph Now Willing to Trust God.* "Thou hast holden my right hand." God was with him throughout his days of doubt, and held him back from catastrophe. "Thou shalt guide me with thy counsel." Now Asaph will listen to the words of God as his Teacher and Friend. "My flesh and my heart faileth" as age creeps on, but what does it matter? "God is the strength of my heart, and my portion forever." He has God, and that is having all. "Whom have I in heaven but thee? and there is none upon earth that I desire beside thee." He is filled with the fulness of God, according to Paul's prayer for the Ephesians. Now he knows that God is good to him and to all the true Israel. "It is good for me to draw near unto God; I have made the Lord God my refuge, that I may tell of all thy works."

(c) *And God Will Receive Him to Glory.* "Thou wilt guide me with thy counsel," he says, "and afterwards receive me to glory." This precious hope of life with God after death he cherishes. The hope of immortality is not as clear in the Old Testament as in the New, but it is seen now and then, and certainly here. Malachi says that the Messenger of the Lord (the Messiah) shall sit as a refiner and purifier of silver (Mal. 3:2 f). The refiner of silver sits before the furnace and watches the dross burn out of the molten mass till he sees his own image reflected perfectly. Then he snatches it away, for it is purified. So Jesus watches His people, as they pass through the refiner's fire, for His own image in us. When He sees His image clearly in us, He takes us to be with Him. "We shall be like him, for we shall see him as he is." Wonder of wonders it will be for sinners like us to be conformed to the image of His Son, when we shall see Him "face to face."

VI

THE LIVING SACRIFICE

"I beseech you therefore, brethren, by the mercies of God, to present your bodies a living sacrifice, holy, acceptable to God, your rational service."—ROMANS 12:1.

THERE is a prejudice today against the word sacrifice, but Paul uses it here in the metaphorical sense for consecration to the service of God. For some it is harder to go on living than to die. The suicide is a coward as well as mentally unbalanced. When Halley's Comet appeared, in 1910, a man in Bowling Green, Kentucky, became so frightened at the stories about hydrocyanic gas in the comet's tail, that he leaped out of a fourth story window to escape the comet. In the early centuries, the *parabolani* (the riskers) courted martyrdom rather than live heroically. The other extreme is to regard religion as a soft snap, a pious feather-bed or asylum.

1. Paul's Appeal to Life.

The first eleven chapters of Romans give a wonderful discussion of the great doctrine of the God-kind of righteousness. Paul has shown its necessity for both Gentiles and Jews, and its nature as purely of grace on the basis of Christ's atoning death, and obtained by faith. Abraham is a fine illustration, for he believed God before he was circumcised. But justification, being set right with God, should lead to sanctification, a progressive process of likeness to Christ. Even the rejection of the Jews will redound to God's glory in the end. Now Paul, as is customary with him in his Epistles, turns to practical exhortations on the basis of the previous massive argument: "I beseech you therefore." Paul's "therefores" are always impressive, and not merely mechanical expletives, as is sometimes the case with preachers. Paul does not discount doctrine or life. It is a false alternative to pit one against the other. He wants the great doctrines applied to life. Christianity is both creed and conduct. The conduct is proof of the creed, as John the Baptist preached: "Bring forth fruits worthy of repentance." Jesus applied the Sermon on the Mount to His hearers, with the saying about the one who hears and does His words. "By their fruits ye shall know them."

2. The Ground of the Appeal.

"By the mercies of God." Paul uses as his "fulcrum" (Moule) "the depth of God's riches." In II Corinthians 1:3 Paul speaks of "the Father of mercies and the God of all consolation." The message of the mercies of God speaks to us out of the great love of God, as shown in the climax of Paul's argument just before: "Oh, the depth of the riches both of the wisdom and knowledge of God! How unsearchable are his judgments, and past tracing out his ways!" (Rom.

11:33). We need the word "untrackable" to express the idea. Some of God's steps can be traced in the history of man and the universe, but many of them are beyond our knowing, too deep and too high for us. But we can trust God's knowledge, power, and love when we cannot see. The sun shines on over us when we are in the fog or the storm. "Our Father knows." We can go on counting our mercies when trouble comes. We can assume, as a matter of course, the mercy of God even in the direst calamity. The old negro's philosophy is not far wrong: "It mout be wuss." So Paul here pleads that we hear the appeal of God's mercies in His plan of redemption through Christ, and in our own experiences. What have we done to show our appreciation of God's mercies to us?

3. The Whole Self at the Service of God.

Their bodies are to be presented to God, not just their spirits. Some of the Gnostics held that the body did not matter, provided they served God with the soul. There are plenty of so-called Christians today, who let the devil have their bodies and seek to serve God with their spirits. The devil in the end will get both soul and body. A wicked man in Chicago in his will left his soul to the devil. He already had it. The body is meant for the temple of the Holy Spirit. "Ye are not your own; ye were bought with a price; glorify God therefore in your body" (I Cor. 6:19-20). So then we are to "present" once for all our bodies here and now, not at death like the usual sacrifice of animals, but our live bodies, a living sacrifice, as an offering of gratitude, not as a means of propitiation. One of the tragedies in the ruins of Jericho and other old cities is to find jars with the bones of little children put in as live sacrifices, when a new house was erected, to propitiate the god of the home.

Our God calls for the offering of the life, not by killing the body but by making the body live for Him, "for this is your rational (or spiritual) service." It is only by the use of the reason that we can control the body. There is no support here for the false views of Freud and other psycho-analysts, that the body's impulses must be given free rein for expression. That way lies animalism, sensuality, gluttony, drunkenness, debauchery, slavery. Paul's plea is for religion to control the body. This is the only way to get a firm basis for ethics. Without God, men like Bertrand Russell and Walter Lippman flounder in a bog to find a basis for the moral life. Paul pleads that we surrender both soul and body unto God, not the soul without the body but the body by the control of the soul. In a word, we are to give God our whole lives. Christ wants all of each of us. Then He will dwell in our hearts by faith and rule our spirits and our bodies.

4. Non-conformity With the World.

"And do not have the habit of following the fashion of this age." It is the present tense of habitual action that is here prohibited by the compound verb *sunschēmatizesthe,* that occurs in the New Testament only here and in I Peter 1:14: "Not fashioning yourselves according to your former lusts in your time of ignorance." Here, "this age" occurs in place of "your time of ignorance," but the idea is practically the same. The distinction between "this age" and "the coming age" occurs in Matthew 12:32 and Ephesians 1:21. In Galatians 1:4 Paul speaks of "this present evil age." Before conversion, Christians "walked according to the age of this world" (Eph. 2:2), but now the wicked world should not set the fashion-plate (*schēma,* our scheme). "The fashion of this world passes by" (I Cor. 7:31), and changes in dress, ideals, and moral standards with each year. Paul is not talking about styles of dress for men or women, but of conduct. The servant of God is to set the standard for the world around him, and not follow the whims and sins of the world.

A practical test for every Christian is presented every day, when he is in a circle that does what his conscience does not approve. Some years ago at the Congress of Mothers in Chicago, the President of the Congress said in a speech that the demi-monde of Paris set the fashions in dress for the women of the world. Do Christian men and women of any city mould the moral life of that city? Do the movies reflect the ethical standards of the nation, or the mercenary motives of corporations that cater to the lowest tastes for revenue? The morals of the movies may shape the lives of the young more powerfully than the home and the Church, if allowed to go on unchecked. There is perpetual conflict between the ideals of Christ and the way of the world in business, in society, in politics, in national government. There is no escape from the demand of the Golden Rule and the social gospel. Some preachers today do not preach the gospel of grace, but only the social gospel. That is putting the cart before the horse. The only way to get the social gospel into effect is to get people converted and determined to be a force for righteousness.

5. Transformation of the Life.

"But be ye transformed by the renewing of your mind." It is the present tense again and means "a perpetual progression, a growth, not so much into grace as in it" (Moule). It is the word used of the transfiguration of Jesus on the mountain (Matt. 17:2), and by Paul in II Corinthians 3:18: "But we all, with unveiled face beholding the glory of the Lord, are being transformed from glory to glory, as by the Spirit of the Lord." It is a radical change of heart and life that is here called for, and not a mere change of fashion. Regeneration (the new birth) is included, but it is more than that. The child grows into manhood by continual progress. "The surrender in purpose becomes a long series of deepening surrenders in habit and action, and a larger discovery of self and of the Lord" (Moule). There is a sharp difference here between "fashion" (*schēma*) and "form" (*morphē*), as in Philippians 2:7. We should be so thoroughly and so continually renewed in mind, that people will see a growing likeness to Christ in us. They will take knowledge of us, that we have been with Jesus. This imitation of Christ is not to be a mere copying of His words and deeds, but an inward approval and expression of the life of Christ within us and without us. We shall walk even as Jesus walked (I John 2:6), because Christ so lives in us that He controls and leads us. "No longer do I live, but Christ lives in me" (Gal. 2:20). This is what Paul means when he tells the Corinthians: "Ye are an epistle of Christ" (II Cor. 3:3). This is the epistle of Christ that people read. They judge the claims of Christ to be what He says He is, by the result in us who say that we are followers of Christ. It is a severe test of the character of each of us, but an inescapable one.

6. Disclosing God's Will by the Life.

"That you may prove what is the will of God, the good and well-pleasing and perfect will." To be sure, God's will is revealed in the Scriptures and in the person, life, and teaching of His Son, Jesus Christ. There are the great facts on record for all, but the average man meets day by day those who profess to have had a change of heart. Is there a change of conduct that corresponds with the renewing of the mind? Does the fig tree have only leaves? The acid test of the life that now is confronts us all. The verb here rendered "prove" means originally to test as metals, to tell gold from fool's gold. Then approval follows, if the test turns out right. So in Philippians 1:10 we have: "That you may distinguish the things that differ," or "that you may approve the things that are excellent." "Try me," says God. Put God's will to the test in your own life. Then you will know by experience how good and perfect and well-pleasing it is. Then we shall disclose God's will in our own lives so as to win others to His service. But we must do God's will in order to put it to the true test, not once or twice, but continually. It is a struggle often for the wilful child to yield to the will of father or mother. But the child that does not learn to do that will be ruined for life, and give untold misery to all concerned. The Lord chastens every son whom He loves, and that child of God by and by enjoys the peaceable fruit of righteousness (Heb. 12:9-11).

The highest test of any life is doing the will of God. To do that one must be yielded to that will, and follow God's guidance, as seen in the Scriptures and in the leading of the Holy Spirit. Then, if one follows the way that God shows him, he will have the richest and most fruitful life and one full of pure joy. It was so with Jesus. When the disciples were amazed that He did not eat the food they brought, He said: "My food is to do the will of him that sent me and to perfect his work." That joy is open to us all if we keep ourselves in tune with God so that we can hear His voice. It is a sad commentary upon one's attitude towards the will of God, when one acts as the friends of Paul did at Cæsarea after Agabus had dramatically warned Paul of what was before him. They besought him with weeping not to go on to Jerusalem, but he insisted: "For I am ready not to be bound only, but also to die at Jerusalem for the name of the Lord Jesus" (Acts 21:13). Then they became silent, saying: "Let the will of the Lord be done." If they could not have their own way, they were reluctantly willing to acquiesce in the will of the Lord. That is better than persistent resistance, but falls very far short of the high ideal here placed before us, of joy in the Lord because we have surrendered our wills to Him. James insists that in all our plans, whether for business or pleasure, we should say, "If the Lord will" (5:15). So Paul purposed to come back to Ephesus, "God willing" (Acts 18:21). This should be our attitude always. We are not to use the phrase as a formula, nor is it always necessary to utter the thought. It is the attitude of heart that matters. "Not my will, but thine, be done" (Luke 22:42), Jesus prayed in Gethsemane.

VII

JESUS WATCHING THE FARMER

A Sermon for Country Life Sunday *

I WAS born and reared in the country, as most preachers are, and know by actual experience the problems of country life which were acute in Virginia and North Carolina in the Reconstruction Period after the Civil War. I had to work on the farm, which was a great blessing to me, and I gained a hunger for knowledge because of the difficulty of securing it. I have also had, during my connection with the seminary, ten years of experience as pastor of three country and village churches in Kentucky (Newcastle, New Salem, Pleasureville). Certainly I learned much myself from this actual contact with country life. I came to love the people, and to see their points of view on many things. I saw at first-hand the joys and the hardships of country church work.

It was before the days of the automobile and of good roads, when the buggy, the horse and the

* A talk over WHAS under the auspices of the Rural Church Commission of Kentucky, 8:30 A.M., May 6, 1934. This was almost certainly the last new sermon Dr. Robertson made.

wagon were the only alternatives to walking. There was no rural free delivery and few telephones and no radios.

But the church was the centre of the life in the country, and the preacher had to preach a real sermon if he could. Dr. Broadus used to say that a theological student, if going to a city church, must take his best coat; but if going to a country church, must take his best sermon. It is doubtful if today the city preacher exerts as profound a moulding influence on the lives of people as the best country preacher does.

Today the automobile makes it possible for the country people to pass by the little country church for the city church, and for city people to pass by any church for golf or for a spin into the country. It was never so important as now for the country preacher to be a man of power, of consecration, of leadership in all phases of country life, for he has much competition. The country church is still the backbone of the religious and social life of the country, and needs a real man to guide it.

Let us think now of JESUS WATCHING THE FARMER.

"*Behold, the sower went forth to sow.*"—Mark 4:3.

We know that the Master was keenly interested in every phase of country life. His boyhood was spent in the village of Nazareth as a carpenter, but He was in constant contact with the open life in the country.

He learned and taught the lesson of the lilies, of the sparrow, of the sower in the field. Many of the parables of Jesus are drawn from His observation of the life of the country people around Nazareth. He often saw the sower go forth into the field and scatter the seed over the land. Some fell by the wayside and the birds quickly picked it up, like the careless listeners at church today. Some fell on rocky ground and sprouted rapidly because of the shallow soil, but soon withered away before the heat of the sun, like the emotional, effervescent people today, who do not hold out. Some fell among thorns and started to grow, but the thorns soon choked the feeble stalks, like the cares of the world and the deceitfulness of riches that gnaw at the souls of men in our own day. Then again Jesus likened the growth of the kingdom of heaven in the heart to the mystery of life as seen in the change of the seed to the stalk, to the flower, to the fruit—a mystery that the farmer does not understand, though all his toil depends on it. And who does truly understand this mystery of life? The tiny mustard seed grows into a bush like a tree large enough for the birds to lodge in. That is the picture of the growth of God's kingdom.

Jesus had often noticed the tares growing in the midst of the wheat in the field, so that the farmer had to leave it till the harvest time, when the separation would be made. Just so in the world, both country and city, bad people live among the good, in spite of churches, schools, government officers: but the day of separation will come in the end. All the same, our task is to hold down the proportion of tares as much as possible, for wheat is the crop desired. There is no danger of an over-supply of this crop of wheat.

The Master had observed the lazy way in which some men did their plowing; they occasionally looked back to see if they were making a straight row, a sure way to make it crooked. Some even gave it up in disgust, not fit for the kingdom of God. There was also the rich fool, whose crops overflowed his barns, while people were in dire need. This rich man was wholly selfish and materialistic, and cared only for bigger barns for his bigger crops, and tried to feed his soul on these material comforts, till the call came for his soul to render an account—like the sudden collapse in 1929 when the bubble of speculation burst. This rich fool had to leave all his "goods" with no "good" in them for him or for any one.

The labourers in the vineyard, who toiled all the day, murmured exceedingly because they did not receive more pay than those who only came to work at the eleventh hour. Jesus had noticed the complaints between employer and employed (our capital and labour problem), and told this story to illustrate His saying about the first being last and the last first. It is not always so, but sometimes it turns out that way. God is sovereign, and knows the motives of people who care more for pay than for the welfare of the kingdom of God. The farmer has much to contend with in the uncertainty of the seasons, the fickleness of the labourers, the fluctuating prices for his produce, but he can, at least, make his own living at home and be independent to that extent, if he knows how to keep out of debt.

Sometimes Jesus noted how the labourers in the vineyard grew restless if the landlord was absent for long, rebelled against the collectors for the rent and slew them, and even dared to kill the son in order to get the whole estate—a striking parallel to the proletariat uprising in Russia today. Jesus several times called attention to the growth of the fig tree as a sign of spring, and noted the barrenness of one that had leaves and no figs. The tree is known by its fruit, whether good or bad. He commented on the eagerness of farmers who watched signs of the weather at sunset or sunrise. In particular, Jesus observed the habit of the shepherd, who knew his sheep by name and would leave the ninety and nine in the fold and go out on the mountain to find the one lost lamb and bring it home on his shoulders. The goats were allowed to run with the sheep by day, but at night they were separated, the sheep going to the right and the goats to the left. Jesus called Himself the Good Shepherd and in the great picture of the Judgment, in Matthew 25, describes Himself as separating the sheep from the goats at last—some goats having passed as sheep and some sheep thinking they were goats.

Jesus saw clearly the inter-relation of farmers with each other. One sows and another reaps. It is a poor farmer who destroys all the timber and wears his land out and lets it all wash away, so that his children have only gullies and rocks from which to get a living. City and country are more linked together in modern life than ever before. Each can ruin the other and each can bless the other. The city pours its vices into the country. The country furnishes the stability of character for the city.

The Master saw the opportunity of the farmer when the fields were ripe for the harvest. It was time to put in the sickle and not to lose the harvest. Laziness and shiftlessness have no place in the country or in the city, but the hobo is fonder of the city than of the country.

Jesus watches the farmer now to see if he can adapt himself to modern conditions and retain the old-fashioned virtues of industry, piety, stability, dependability and independence, along with the demand for co-operation, sympathy, enlightenment, and progress.

O God of our fathers, bless those who still live in the open spaces of our land, away from the crowds and strife of our cities. May they find Thee near always in the life all about them, life from the touch of Thy hand. Grant Thy blessing to the country homes, that fathers and mothers may reverence Thee and rear their children in the love and worship of Almighty God. May the country boys and girls still be the greatest crop raised on the farm. May they become noble men and women, strong in character, forward-looking, eager to serve God and man anywhere and everywhere, able to conserve the best in the life of the world, and to enrich it with high thinking and high deeds. Amen.

VIII

A RICH ENTRANCE INTO HEAVEN

"For thus shall be richly supplied unto you the entrance into the eternal kingdom of our Lord and Saviour Jesus Christ."—II Peter 1:11.

THIS opening paragraph is rich in spiritual insight and worthy of Simon Peter. Many have doubts concerning the genuineness of II Peter. It claims to be by the Apostle Peter, and so is not anonymous. If not authentic, then it is pseudonymous; but certainly it is far superior to the pseudonymous writings. There are difficulties of style, but the balance is still in favour of the genuineness of the Epistle. If I did not think so, I would not preach from it. Some reject it because Jesus is called God in 1:1: "Our God and Saviour Jesus Christ." The Greek idiom compels this reading. John applies the word "God" to Jesus in the first verse of his Gospel, as Paul does in Titus 2:13. This paragraph in two long sentences graphically pictures God's dealing with His people, the elect, the believers.

1. God's Call and Promise.

God has called us (1:3), "by his own glory and virtue," that is, as manifested in the Lord Jesus Christ.

He has shown His love for us in Christ, and His divine power has bestowed on us all that we need for full knowledge of Christ, in order to resist all the subtleties of the Gnostics and all other specious heretics like the so-called Christian Scientists today. It is unusual to find the word "virtue" applied to God, for it is a human virtue. Perhaps Peter is insisting thus indirectly on the real humanity of Christ, as against the Docetic Gnostics who denied it. But God has also granted unto us "his exceeding great and precious promises," to steady us and to establish, "that by means of these ye may become partakers of the divine nature." This phrase, "the divine nature," "belongs rather to Hellenism than to the Bible" (Bigg), but Gnosticism, which Peter is opposing as Paul and John did, adopted many Greek ideas. Peter adapts his language to meet their contentions. He refers to regeneration, as in I Peter 1:23, and to constant growth as children of God (I Pet. 2:1 f). This is a common idea in the New Testament, and one that needs emphasis now. Having been born again, we have the glorious privilege of growing into full manhood in Christ Jesus our Lord (Eph. 4:15). Man, with his moral nature, is capable of sinking to the level of the devil, like Judas Iscariot, or of rising higher than the angels into the likeness of God in Christ (Rom. 8:29), our Elder Brother (Heb. 2:11 f). We are heirs of the promises of God, co-heirs with Christ, destined to share in the glory of Christ (Rom. 8:17), and in some true sense to be like Christ (I John

3:2). All this, and more, is involved in God's call and promise to those who obtain a like precious faith with us in the righteousness of our God and Saviour Jesus Christ.

2. God's Demand from Us.

But salvation is not a one-sided affair. God takes the initiative. He first loved us, and proved His unmatched love by the unspeakable gift of His Son to be the Redeemer and Saviour of all who will believe on Him. God's call and precious promises do not serve as a narcotic or a soporific. We are not to lull ourselves to idle complacency because of the wonders of God's grace and love, as shown in Jesus Christ. He has provided "all things for life and godliness," but His surpassing grace calls for a response on our part. We are not to sin that grace may the more abound, as Paul ably showed in Romans 6, nor are we to remain idle and shrivel into atrophy. "For this very reason" (I Pet. 1:5), the greatness of God's gracious love to us in Christ, we are called upon to lay hold ourselves: "Do you add on your part all zeal." "The soul of religion is the practical part," says Bunyan. Peter here touches our own duty to God. We are to bring in alongside of God's plan and purpose "all zeal," diligence, speed, haste to carry out God's purpose in our lives. Peter uses the word "supply" in explaining what the Christian is expected to do. The word *epichorigeō* originally means that the leader of a chorus supplied the equipment necessary. The state (in

Athens) secured the chorus and the leader furnished the outfit needed. So, to carry on Peter's metaphor, God has selected each of us, but we have a part to play also.

Peter fills in the list of details that belong to our part of the performance, the human side. They are linked together like a chain or, better still, one rises upon the other like the steps in a stairway. There are frequent lists of virtues in the New Testament like Galatians 5:22 f. Paul alludes to his progress in Judaism as a youth (Gal. 1:14), and urges Timothy to practise his gifts, "that thy progress may be manifest to all" (I Tim. 4:15). Peter suggests faith as the first thing that we are to supply. This is the root of the Christian life on the human side (Eph. 2:8), if we think of a tree; the first stone if we think of a pillar, a tower, a house. God gives us a new heart, and we respond with trust, which becomes the guarantee or title-deed (Heb. 11:1) to all the rest. The next step above faith is virtue, used of God (in verse 3); here of man the expression in conduct of the faith, the moral power that regulates the life. "One step leads to another, and each step is made by the co-operation of the human will with the divine" (Bigg). After virtue comes knowledge, insight, understanding, intelligence, by experience of grace in its application to life. Some take it here to mean "practical skill in the details of Christian duty." Most of all, knowledge of Christ, and experience of His power through the Holy Spirit.

The Christian needs the clearest intelligence and the utmost trust combined, as he confronts the temptations and tasks of life. The next step called for is self-control. The word literally means holding in, just the opposite of the *libido* commended by Freud and his followers. It is folly to propose license (licentiousness) as superior to self-control, self-mastery. It still is better to rule one's self than to master a city, and often more difficult, severe as that task is.

Control does not mean indulgence. There is a new scorn developed about liquor, that one is not temperate who does not drink at all; that the really temperate man is the one who drinks and is able to stop before drunk. There might be some point in that argument if alcohol were a food instead of a poison. One may as well argue that one should use morphine, or any other poisonous drug in moderation, to show that he can stop in time. Modern science and human history advocate abstinence from alcohol as the only safe way of maintaining self-control, whether driving an automobile or living a life. Next to self-control comes patience. This grace means remaining under the burden without complaining, standing in one's lot and doing the duty of the hour, and finding joy in the midst of tribulations that may surround one (I Pet. 1:6), however varied and manifold they may be. One is getting on in grace when he reaches this stage.

Next comes godliness, already named in verse 3, which means worship of God, the spirit of reverence and adoration of Almighty God, "a large word, summing up the whole of the practical side of the Christian life" (Bigg). Irreverence is one of the vices of modern life. The next step is brotherly love. This love of the brethren is like the second commandment of Jesus, to love our neighbours as we do ourselves. It here follows godliness, which means the first, to love God with all the mind and heart. If all nominal Christians really loved one another, strife would disappear from neighbourhoods and churches, and peace would reign among men of goodwill. The climax of it all is love; love without definition, love for Christ, love for all men, love that abides forever with faith and hope, and that is greatest of all (I Cor. 13:13). Jesus Christ is the measure of God's love for the world (John 3:16). He is the challenge of our love for God and men.

3. God's Expectation from Us.

Peter presents the picture of these noble graces in full measure. "If these things are yours and abound," he says. The word here means "increasing," rather than "abounding." A healthy tree that bears abundant fruit is continually growing. "They make you to be not idle nor unfruitful unto the knowledge of our Lord Jesus Christ." In Colossians 1:10 Paul has a similar statement: "Bearing fruit in every good work, and increasing in the knowledge of God." Here the full knowledge of God is the outcome of all our strivings and of God's blessing, like the prayer in Ephesians 3:19, and like Peter's exhortation in II Peter 3:18:

"Grow in the grace and knowledge of our Lord and Saviour Jesus Christ." But this knowledge of Christ is the root of all that follows, and that may be the idea here. Rooted and builded up in Christ (Col. 2:7), the disciple will not be idle or unfruitful. The Master says that the one who abides in Him bears much fruit (John 15:5).

In contrast with this happy ideal, Peter describes the false teachers (Gnostics): "For he to whom these things are not present is blind, seeing only what is near." They are unfruitful like barren trees (Luke 13:6), and blind leaders of the blind, all falling into the ditch (Matt. 15:14). The word here for near-sightedness (*muōpazō*) means to screw up the eyes because of the light, to blink the eyes and turn them away from the light and so to see only what is quite near, to get a short-sighted and imperfect view. What a vivid picture of so many who cannot endure the full glory of Jesus, the Light of the world, those whom the god of this world has blinded (II Cor. 4:4). Such a short-sighted man may even be one who has forgotten the cleansing of his sins and has returned, like the dog to his vomit, and like the sow, to wallowing in the mire (II Pet. 2:22).

Meanwhile, and wherefore also, Peter exhorts his readers to renewed zeal: "Be zealous to make your calling and election sure." He does not look on election as an excuse for inaction, but as an incentive and a spur to activity to carry out the will of God. "For doing these things ye shall never stumble." Peter could speak feelingly on the subject of stumbling, for he had once done his share. But he had turned, and Jesus had charged him to strengthen his brethren, and that he is here doing. Peter's theology on this point is in perfect accord with that of Paul in Philippians 2:12 f: "With fear and trembling work out your own salvation, for God is the one who works in you of his own good pleasure, both the willing and the doing." Here are both sides of the truth, like the old negro's exegesis: "I ain' never know anybody git 'lected what didn' run!"

4. God's Abundant Reward for Us.

God took pity on us. He first loved us and gave His Son for us to be our Saviour. But He expects us to meet and match His love with a life of service that ripens into the rich graces from faith to love, and to do it with heartiness and enthusiasm. If we do our part in this fashion "thus," "there will be richly supplied unto you the entrance into the eternal kingdom of our Lord and Saviour Jesus Christ." There is only one way of being saved, and that is by faith in Jesus Christ as our Saviour from sin. But rewards are bestowed according to the quality and quantity of the service rendered, not according to one's reputation among men. The record of each of us is in the Book of Life. Paul speaks of one's being saved so as by fire (I Cor. 3:15), the man himself being saved by grace and his works burned up, being wood, hay, stubble and not able to stand the test of fire. God furnishes the welcome in accord with the actual character wrought. It is not unseemly that the heavenly chorus should greet a Paul, a Luther, a Spurgeon, a William Booth. Most of us will be content to slip in quietly the way that John Jasper dreamed it would be, when he would "sit and gaze for ten thousand years at Jesus." But the word "richly" here suggests another way of entering in. A ship may barely reach the harbour after many storms and perils, after mutiny and famine, with all the cargo gone, almost a wreck. Another ship may sweep in with full cargo, after storm and battle, with all the sails flying, and be welcomed with "Well done, thou faithful servant."

IX

THE DAWNING OF NEW TRUTH

"Of a truth I perceive that God is not a respecter of persons."—ACTS 10:34.

PETER came to see this new truth with great difficulty, and the perception of it caused an intellectual revolution in his mind and attitude toward Gentiles. Peter's experience is well worth the serious study of modern men.

1. Peter in the Grip of the Prejudices of a Lifetime.

Like all Jews, he knew that Israel was the chosen people of God, chosen, many held, as alone constituting the Kingdom of God. The rabbis carried this idea so far as to consider all Jews heirs of God by birth because descendants of Abraham. John the Baptist bluntly termed the Pharisees and Sadducees "offspring of vipers," and denied that salvation was a matter of national inheritance: "Think not to say within yourselves, We have Abraham as father, for I tell you that God is able out of these stones to raise up children to Abraham" (Matt. 3:9). But the Pharisees and Sadducees were not convinced by the Baptist, for they rejected his baptism and his teaching. Jesus Himself endorsed this fierce judgment of the Baptist and likewise called the religious leaders "offspring of vipers" (Matt. 12:34). Jesus had said: "Other sheep I have which are not of this fold" (John 10:16), and that by the Cross He would draw all men to Him (John 12:32). After His resurrection He had given the great commission to carry the gospel unto all nations (Matt. 28:19), "unto the uttermost part of the earth" (Acts 1:8).

Peter himself, under the illumination of the Holy Spirit on the great day of Pentecost, had boldly proclaimed: "For to you is the promise and to your children and to all those afar off, as many as the Lord our God calls to himself" (Acts 2:39). But it seems clear that Peter understood his own words to mean that the Gentiles thus called would also become Jews as well as Christians. Certainly that is not the meaning or purpose of the Master, but Peter, along with the other early Christians, was a Jew and looked on other peoples as "afar off." The middle wall of partition in the temple kept the Gentiles in the Court of the Gentiles, and symbolized the cleavage between Jews and Gentiles all over the world in religion and social life. Peter, now the leader of the Christians in Jerusalem, had not yet seen that this middle wall of partition between Jew and Gentile was broken down in Christ, as Paul came to see it (Eph. 1:13-18). The Samaritans had received the gospel with the approval of Peter and John, but they had been circumcised and so were technically Jews, though cordially hated by the Jews. The eunuch from Ethiopia was an exceptional case and was apparently a proselyte.

Peter was already violating one of the prejudices of the strict Jews in stopping in the house of a tanner in Joppa, whose business was considered unclean. But even so, he was wholly unprepared to accept the Lord's invitation to stay and eat the unclean animals in the vision on the housetop in Joppa. He recognized the vision as from God and the command as God's, and yet he dared to say: "By no means, Lord; because never yet did I eat anything common or unclean" (Acts 10:14). No more striking illustration of the blinding and binding power of custom and prejudice can be imagined than this. Even the clear voice of God in explanation failed to shake Peter's stand: "The things which God cleansed do not thou treat as common." The vision was repeated three times, with the command of God likewise, and yet Peter did not obey. He was, to be sure, at a loss in himself what the vision which he had seen might mean (Acts 10:17), but he was unable to reconcile this new command of God with the former commands of God concerning unclean animals. He did not yet perceive the bearing of the vision on the mission of Christ to men of all races. Those whom Luke in Acts calls Judaizers, those

Christians of the circumcision who insisted to the end that Gentiles could not be saved without becoming Jews, were never able to see what the Samaritans long ago had seen, that Jesus was the Saviour of the world (John 4:42). They remained reactionaries, and fought Paul bitterly for preaching Christ among the Gentiles, without making them Jews also. Peter was in trouble over the vision and wanted more light. He was willing to follow, and God led him.

2. Peter in a New Environment.

Peter kept revolving in his mind the problem of the vision and his own conduct concerning it (Acts 10:19). He was quite prepared for more light about it, when the Holy Spirit expressly told him that two (three, according to some manuscripts) men were seeking him and that he was to go with them "nothing doubting." But he was not told where he was to go nor what he was to do. He was led on gradually in the radical readjustment that was to come. So he listened to the message of Cornelius, brought by these men, and welcomed them into the house, though apparently Gentiles. The next day he went with them, but took the precaution to take along with him six Jewish Christians from Joppa, as a guarantee in case of trouble (10:23, 45; 11:12). That was ordinary prudence, for, though directly commanded by the Holy Spirit, his experience with the vision made him feel the need of human sympathy and co-operation, in case he was placed in a predicament. He knew now that he was going to a Roman centurion, though apparently a "proselyte of the Gate," a God-fearer and open to the gospel.

On his arrival he went boldly into the house of Cornelius, though fully aware that it was an unusual, not to say unlawful, thing for a pious Jew to do. An instance of this seclusiveness of the Jews appears in the refusal of the Sanhedrin to enter Pilate's palace at the trial of Jesus (John 18:28). Peter found a considerable company of the family and friends of Cornelius gathered in the house, but he had crossed the Rubicon and must make the best of it. He called attention to the boldness of what he had done, as they well understood, and now he himself saw a great light. He began to understand the meaning of the vision on the housetop in Joppa: "But unto me God showed that I should not call any man common or unclean" (10:28). Here he is in the house of a Gentile, a thing worse than eating the unclean food that God had invited him to do. It is significant that Peter did not see the meaning of the vision till he was on the inside of the house of Cornelius, the Gentile. That is often true, and it renders it important where one goes for his education, his work, his pleasure, his worship. It is the experience of many a student that the college changes his whole outlook on life for better or worse, as the case may be. That fact imposes a tremendous responsibility on the teacher to give the students the truth, not guesses, so far as he is able to do so. If the new view is mere hypothesis, it should be presented in that light and not as fact. On the other hand, the student needs an open mind for the reception of the truth, without injury to his ideals and standards. Harm often comes when a daredevil teacher confronts a reactionary student. In this case Cornelius commends Peter for coming to him, Gentile as he is, for both Cornelius and Peter had been prepared by God for each other: "Now therefore we are all here present in the sight of God, to hear all things commanded thee by the Lord" (10:33). That is the proper attitude for learning, and it offers Peter an unparalleled opportunity, provided he has himself the right message for this new situation.

Peter faces the first Gentile audience ever confronted by a preacher of Christ. The thousands converted under his ministry at the great Pentecost were Jews from all parts of the world. But here are Romans, prepared for the knowledge of Christ. What has Peter to say to them? Shall he insist on Moses as the way to Christ? Shall he assume that Gentiles can come directly to Christ? Is the gospel of Christ for Gentiles, as well as for Jews, without their becoming Jews? Is Peter equal to this situation, as he was by the help of the Holy Spirit in Jerusalem? Not unless he has learned the lesson of the vision in Joppa. It is a crisis for Peter and for Christianity.

3. Peter Accepting the New Truth of Gentile Freedom.

He opened his mouth to speak, and his first utterance revealed that the light was shining in his mind and heart: "Of a truth I perceive that God is not a respecter of persons; but in every nation the one who fears him and works righteousness is acceptable to him" (10:34). This great truth he now perceives and boldly proclaims. The middle wall of partition is now gone for Simon Peter: "Jesus is Lord of all," of Gentiles as well as Jews. This is the word of God, as witnessed by the prophets concerning the Messiah, "that through his name every one who believes on him should receive remission of sins." So Peter preaches salvation through Christ to these Romans, the same gospel of grace for all. He does not mean that God has another way of salvation for the heathen, through Confucius, Buddha, Mohammed. That is not the new truth that has dawned upon Peter. He tells these Romans not about the beauty of Stoicism or Epicureanism or Platonism, but he gives them in summary fashion the story of the life, death, and resurrection of Jesus Christ, precisely as do missionaries today in heathen lands. Peter speaks as a personal witness of Jesus Christ, as the Master has commanded. A witness tells what he knows, not what he has heard. The new thing about it now is that Peter tells this same story to the Gentiles. It is a new experience for Peter, this thing of preaching to the Gentiles, but he put his heart into it. He believed that he was telling them the things commanded by the Lord. A preacher has no business preaching anything else. His guesses he can keep to himself. The pulpit is no place for them.

4. The Seal of God's Blessing Upon the Message.

Peter was certain that God had opened this door through which he had entered, but he was not quite prepared for the sudden turn that things took. He was hardly through with his discourse about Jesus, when all of a sudden the Holy Spirit fell upon all those who heard the Word. They began to speak with tongues, as the disciples did at the great Pentecost, and to magnify God. The six disciples from Joppa "were astonished that the gift of the Holy Spirit had been poured out even upon the Gentiles." Peter stopped his sermon and boldly asked: "Can any one forbid water that these, who received the Holy Spirit even as we also, should not be baptized?" In this case the Holy Spirit came upon the Gentiles before baptism. So Peter gave orders that they should be baptized, apparently by the six Jewish brethren from Joppa. The Gentiles now had a church, a Roman church, in Cæsarea. It was a Gentile Pentecost. God had cleared the doubt from Peter's mind. The puzzle was solved. Gentiles are saved, just as Jews are, by faith in Jesus Christ as Lord and Saviour. Peter had followed God's leading, and he now saw clearly. He had taken his stand in the front of one of the great revolutions of history, the giving the gospel to the Gentiles. This new truth works. Present-day civilization rests upon it.

5. Peter Paying the Penalty for Accepting the Truth.

The apostles and the brethren in all Judæa heard the wonderful news "that even the Gentiles received the word of God" (11:1). No effort was made to make them Jews. Apparently there was rejoicing over this new step. But on Peter's return to Jerusalem the party of the circumcision, a Pharisaic group in the church there (15:5), were greatly displeased and challenged Peter, not about his preaching or the conversion of the Gentiles, but over his breach of Jewish custom in going into the house of Gentiles and eating with them (11:3). That was a fact, and all the Jewish prejudice about the Gentiles flared up at once.

Peter saw the gravity of the situation and did a masterly thing. He told the story of God's dealing with him at Joppa and in Cæsarea, and called the six Jewish brethren from Joppa to witness to the accuracy of his report (11:12), how the Holy Spirit came upon the Gentiles while he was preaching. In a word, he showed that it was all God's doing, not his. In fact, in his vision at Joppa he had refused to obey the Lord about eating unclean food and only came to Cæsarea and entered the house of Cornelius at the express command of the angel of the Lord who had also prepared Cornelius for this message. "Who was I, able to hinder God?" (11:17). It was a master-stroke and completely answered the critics of Peter's conduct. They all became silent and glorified God: "Well then, even to the Gentiles did God give repentance unto life" (11:18). It was reluctant acquiescence, but inevitable. And yet there was an implied meaning that they would forgive Peter this time, so plainly led of the Lord, but he must not let it happen again.

The first case of church discipline in the Acts is this bringing the chief apostle before the Church for preaching to the Gentiles. But Peter had taken his stand for the freedom that is in Christ. The truth of Christ had set him free, and he was free indeed. Later, when these same Judaizers attack Paul and Barnabas for their campaign among the Gentiles, Peter boldly takes his stand for liberty for the Gentiles (15:7-11), and alludes to his work in Cæsarea. True, in Antioch Peter will flicker in his conduct about this very matter of eating with the Gentiles (Greeks), and will receive a sharp rebuke from Paul for his hypocrisy (Gal. 2:11-13). But this was Peter's cowardice, not change of convictions. The

Judaizers through all the ages have fought to place the yoke of bondage on all Christians. But Christ set us free for freedom (Gal. 5:1). We were called for freedom in Christ. The sun shines for all. Let it shine.

X

POWER AND WITNESS

"But ye shall receive power, the Holy Spirit having come upon you, and ye shall be witnesses of me, both in Jerusalem, and in all Judæa and Samaria, and unto the uttermost part of the earth."—Acts 1:8.

THESE are the last words of the Risen Christ, as He ascended on high from Olivet, before the eyes of the eager and anxious disciples, who were still looking for a political kingdom or revolution. They had regained faith and hope since they had seen Jesus risen from the dead. Despair had changed to hope, and doubt to faith. The radical upheaval and reversal of conditions did not happen because of any preconceived plan or purpose of the disciples. They themselves were the sceptics, the doubters, who were slowly convinced by indubitable proofs from the Master Himself. Christianity was dead, but for the resurrection of Christ. But even so, the disciples were without a programme, without a clear grasp of the meaning of Christ (His person, mission, and message). They had failed to convince Thomas, one of their own number, of the fact of Christ's resurrection, till he saw Jesus for himself. They had received the great commission for world evangelization, but were ill-equipped to carry it into execution. The Master Himself saw that, and provided for it by "the promise of the Father," for which they were to tarry in Jerusalem, till they put on as a new garment ("be clothed with") power from on high, the coming of the Holy Spirit upon them in special power and significance. It is now over nineteen hundred years since the great Pentecost, when the Holy Spirit came and introduced the dispensation of the Spirit, under whose leadership we labour till Jesus comes again. It is always important for us to test ourselves by the great experience of those epochal days in Jerusalem.

1. The Disciples Recognized Their Need.

Jesus had commanded them to wait for the coming of the Holy Spirit upon them. No precise day had been set, only it was to be "not many days hence." They were now without the visible presence of the Master, though He had promised to be with them all the days, that is, through "the other Paraclete" who was to take the place of Christ. They had not understood all that Jesus taught them. They had been particularly dull about His death and resurrection and the spiritual nature of the Kingdom of God. They needed new insight into the meaning of the Cross of Christ, and were not prepared to take the gospel to the nations of the earth, nor even to proclaim it in Jerusalem. They lacked power also to convince others who had doubts and objections, prejudices and various erroneous beliefs. So they were quite willing to wait for the next step in the programme of Christ. They were emptied of self-conceit and self-confidence, and that is always a prerequisite for the incoming of the Holy Spirit into one's heart and life.

These men and women were all converted. They had been begotten again by the Holy Spirit, but they lacked the teaching of the Spirit, who alone can take of the things of Christ and make them ours. It is just here that some schoolmen fail. Intellectual knowledge of the facts about Christ is important, but not enough. One may know all the vast literature about Christ, and yet not know Christ. Criticism of Christ is not surrender to Christ. And one cannot know the teaching of Christ who refuses to do the will of God about Him. The point of contact with Christ is primarily in the heart and will. So the disciples waited in prayer and in faith, waited for ten days in fact, till the day of Pentecost came, fifty days after the crucifixion. They were all there in one place, and were of one accord in their desire to receive the promise of the Father. It is certain that this attitude of united prayer is essential for a spiritual revival for any church and for any age.

They kept vigil with expectancy and with a strange joy, now that Jesus had really gone from them.

They did not know precisely what to expect, and what happened upset them greatly. The signs (sound of a mighty wind, tongues of flame, the speaking in foreign languages) were proofs that the Holy Spirit had come. These signs were not the Spirit. The tongues were understood by various groups, as in Corinth (else, Paul said, they were to be silent). We have no occasion to look for such proofs now, and certainly do not have them in the so-called "tongues" now.

2. The Holy Spirit's Power Seen in Simon Peter.

The people misunderstood the signs, but Peter, now enlightened by the Holy Spirit, interprets this great event as the fulfilment of Joel's prophecy: "This is that spoken by the prophet Joel" (Acts 2:16). He gives a spiritual interpretation of the wonders in the heavens and signs upon the earth, blood and fire and vapour of smoke, the sun turned into darkness and the moon into blood. This exegesis by Peter should give pause to those who insist upon a literal interpretation of Messianic symbolic language. But the significant thing about Peter's discourse is that he is the first one to interpret the mission of Christ under the guidance of the Holy Spirit, the power promised by Jesus. The old misapprehension about a political king and kingdom is gone. It is the Crucified and Risen Christ that has fulfilled prophecy, and is now the hope of all men, who can be saved by faith in Him alone.

A remarkable thing about Peter is his new courage before the people and the Sanhedrin. No denials of his Lord now, but open defiance of the Jewish rulers, and charging them with the death of Jesus, and proclaiming His resurrection, of which Peter is a witness. This new insight and new power remain with Peter, who is now willing to go to prison for Christ in reality, as he had once prematurely boasted. Now that he has the power of the Holy Spirit, he is courageous, not cowardly, a dynamo of energy. Peter now tells the people, who are pierced to the heart, what to do: "Repent, and let each one of you be baptized in the name of Jesus Christ for the forgiveness of your sins, and ye shall receive the gift of the Holy Spirit" (Acts 2:38). This is said to the excited crowds. Turning to Christ would bring forgiveness of sins, and baptism would proclaim in symbolic fashion the new experience of grace. It was a great occasion. No wonder that three thousand believed and were baptized on that day. Peter preached with the power of the Holy Spirit. No other preaching has power with man and from God. Preachers need natural gifts and education, but most of all this supernatural power of the Holy Spirit. The preacher of God's message must be in contact with God to have power with men. That is the explanation of Peter's sermon on this occasion, of Paul's preaching, of Luther, Spurgeon, Moody, Maclaren, Broadus.

3. The Path to Power Today.

There is no doubt that many preachers and Christian workers have lost the evangelistic note and the power of winning souls, by ignoring the Holy Spirit. Some have done this through excessive confidence in their own gifts of scholarship and of eloquence. They feel no need for supernatural help in proclaiming the gospel of Christ. They have had success at other times and in other places, and calmly go through the motions this time and are surprised at the lack of results. They are like the nine disciples who attempted to cast the demon out of the afflicted boy, while Jesus and the other three were on the Mount of Transfiguration. When they asked Jesus for an explanation of their failure, they were told that it was lack of prayer. They had failed to get in touch with God through prayer, and pronounced the words as if they had a magical formula. Their words were empty and powerless. A prayerless preacher is a powerless preacher.

Some are led away by new cults and new fads which have no promise or power in them. Some preachers give the people a rehash of the news in the daily papers or the radio or the movies. There is no power in such sensational newsmongering. Not a few preachers preach socialism in place of the gospel. Christianity leads to brotherly love in its noblest expression of service to hospitals, orphanages, asylums, community chests, and all other forms of social helpfulness. But these things are the expression of Christianity, not the gospel itself. Every great revival springs out of contact with God in Christ through the Holy Spirit. He is the power; not the preacher's personality, not the church, not organization, not money, not numbers, not culture, not scholarship. The people were cut to the heart under Peter's preaching, because he presented Christ as the Risen Lord and Saviour from sin. That message alone will pierce to the hearts of sinners today. And men are sinners today, just as much as in Peter's day, sinners with new turns and charms, but sinners. Modern discoveries and inventions do not change human nature, but play into the hands of gangsters with machine guns and gas bombs, automobiles and airplanes.

Let the Holy Spirit come into your heart and life. Let Him use your gifts and attainments for the glory of God, not for your own promotion. The Holy Spirit can use "unlearned and ignorant men" like Peter and John, or learned men like Paul. He is the power in any man who serves Christ. Organization is good, but power is needed. Machinery is useless without power to make it work. There is constant danger today that we shall be paralyzed by the cumbersome machinery in our modern Christian organizations. The Church of England would not let John Wesley preach in the churches. He used tombstones as pulpits, since the churches were dead. He waked up the dead and saved England from deism and the

French Revolution. The path to power is the path to the throne of God. "I can do all things through the one who keeps on pouring power into me," says Paul (Phil. 4:13). Out of touch with Christ, the preacher is powerless. In touch with Christ, he is irresistible.

4. **Witnesses From Experience.**

It is the preacher who knows Christ best who has most power with men. Moody illustrates what God can do with a man wholly consecrated to Him, a man without the culture of the schools, who yet touched the hearts of the students in Oxford and Cambridge as no other preacher has done. But with the new insight and the new power from the Holy Spirit, the disciples tarried too long in Jerusalem, while Judæa, Samaria, and the uttermost parts of the earth clamoured for the knowledge of Christ. They did have great success in Jerusalem; so much so that the Sadducees persecuted the apostles for preaching the resurrection, and the Pharisees put Stephen to death for proclaiming that men could worship God apart from the temple.

This very persecution, led by the brilliant young Pharisee, the pride of Gamaliel, resulted in the conversion of this most gifted and able Jew of his time, Saul of Tarsus, whose persecution had scattered the saints, and who himself became the chief apostle to the Gentiles. He saw the Risen Christ on the way to Damascus, and became himself the chief witness for Christ throughout the Roman empire. It is to be noted that while the unschooled disciples shook Jerusalem with the power of the Holy Spirit, it was a man of the schools (the seminary of Gamaliel in Jerusalem and possibly the university of Tarsus) who won a hearing for Christ before the Græco-Roman world. But, gifted and cultured as Paul was, he was simply the new agent for the work of the Holy Spirit. Paul spoke from the unshaken conviction that he had seen the Risen Jesus, and hence that Jesus of Nazareth was the Messiah of Jewish hope and promise, the Saviour of sinners, the Son of God and the Son of man, the Lord of all. He was a witness, a flaming torch, whose light still shines across the centuries. The preacher who talks about Christ, without knowing Christ in his own heart, may be orthodox or heretic, but he will be without power and without a hearing. The men of today come like the Greeks of old and say: "Sir, we desire to see Jesus." And we cannot show Jesus to the modern Greeks unless we ourselves have tasted and know that the Lord is gracious.

XI

THE BLESSED HOPE OF CHRIST'S SECOND COMING

"Looking for the blessed hope and appearing of the glory of our great God and Saviour Jesus Christ."—TITUS 2:13.

1. This Blessed Hope Often Misunderstood.

THERE are Christians today who no longer look for or believe in the personal Second Coming of Jesus Christ. Some consider the whole thing a misinterpretation and a misapplication of the language in the New Testament, which only means a general diffusion of Christ's influence in the world. Others bluntly say that the apostles (and even Jesus Himself) were mistaken in expecting and teaching the return of Christ within a few years. They admit that even Christ had a wrong perspective in His eschatology and, like Schweitzer, make the hope of a sudden and supernatural cataclysm the chief element in the teaching of Jesus about His Kingdom. Some who early held this erroneous view soon began to mock and to say: "Where is the promise of his coming? for, from the day that the fathers fell asleep, all things continue as they were from the beginning of the creation" (II Pet. 3:4).

No teaching of the New Testament has received worse treatment than this. On the one hand, there are elaborate programmes arranged for the course of history till the Lord's return, and dates set for that coming, in spite of the Master's express statement that no one save the Father Himself knows when it will be, and that He will come suddenly and unexpectedly, like a thief in the night. On the other hand, many Christians take no real interest in the subject, in spite of the urgent and repeated exhortation of Jesus to be ready: "Watch therefore, for ye know not on what day your Lord cometh" (Matt. 24:42). If we think that the nineteen hundred years that have slipped by are enough to dull the edge of this hope, let us recall Peter's reply to the scoffers: "But forget not this one thing, beloved, that one day is with the Lord as a thousand years, and a thousand years as one day. The Lord is not slack concerning his promise, as some count slackness; but is long-suffering to you-ward, not wishing that any should perish, but that all should come to repentance" (II Pet. 3:8 f.). Clearly, then, neglect of this promise is not the way to treat God's long-suffering. It is worth while to try to understand the teaching of the New Testament about it.

Some scholars see a separation in this sentence in Titus 2:13 between God and Jesus Christ; but the grammar and the context demand one person here, and that person is Jesus Christ, our great God and Saviour. The one article with "God" and "Saviour" demands this view. The word for "appearing" (*epiphaneia*) is never in the New Testament applied to the Father, but only to the Son—once of the Incarnation (II Tim. 1:10), elsewhere of the Second Coming (II Thess. 2:8; I Tim. 6:14; II Tim. 4:1, 8; and here in Titus). The relative clause in verse 14 is only true of Jesus Christ, who gave Himself for us to redeem us from all iniquity. If it is objected that Paul does not elsewhere apply the word "God" (*theos*) to Christ, we may refer to Romans 9:5 (the correct punctuation, "God blessed forever," in apposition with "Christ") and to Paul's address to the Ephesian elders in Acts 20:28, "the church of God which he purchased with his own blood." Besides, in Colossians 1:14-20 Paul uses language of Christ as Creator and Redeemer, tantamount to the word "God," and in 2:9 says pointedly of Christ: "For in him dwelleth all the fulness of the Godhead bodily." Already the Ptolemies and the Roman emperors were constantly called "our great God and Saviour," according to papyri and inscriptions. Paul, like the other Christians, "annexed for their divine Master the phraseology that was impiously arrogated to themselves by some of the worst of men" (James Hope Moulton, *Prolegomena*, page 84). "This text is a direct, definite, and even studied declaration of the divinity of the Eternal Son" (Ellicott). So then, Paul here directly says that Christians of his day were looking for the blessed hope and appearing of our great God and

Saviour Jesus Christ." He appeared once (Titus 2:11; Phil. 2:5-11), and He will appear again in glory.

2. Christ May Come at Any Time.

It is often assumed and stated that Paul held and preached that Jesus would return during his own lifetime, if not almost immediately. It is strange that men today should say this of Paul, in view of his express denial of such a statement in II Thessalonians 2:1 f., "Now we beseech you, brethren, touching the coming of our Lord Jesus Christ, and our gathering together unto him; to the end that ye be not quickly shaken from your mind, nor yet be troubled, either by spirit or by word, or by epistle as from us, as that the day of the Lord is just at hand." Clearly some in Thessalonica had so represented Paul's position, and thus justified their idle habits under the guise of piety, "doing nothing but doing around" (II Thess. 3:10-12). Paul explains that "the falling away" must "come first, and the man of sin be revealed," whatever that means. Some had been honestly troubled for fear that when Christ does appear, the dead in Christ will not see Him. He explained that the dead in Christ would "rise first; then we that are alive, that are left, shall together with them be caught up into the clouds, to meet the Lord in the air; and so shall we ever be with the Lord" (I Thess. 4:16 f.). But Paul did not mean by this language that he himself would certainly be alive at that time. He was alive when he wrote, and so spoke of himself that way. The Thessalonians had no reason for their misunderstanding. "But concerning the times and the seasons, brethren, ye have no need that aught be written unto you. For yourselves know perfectly that the day of the Lord so cometh as a thief in the night" (I Thess. 5:1 f.).

In Philippians 1:21-26, Paul balances life and death in his own case, with the preference for death in order to depart and be with Christ, but willing to remain and labour for his Master, so long as there is work for him to do. This was during his first Roman imprisonment. He still hoped for Christ's Second Coming, as we see in our text, written after his release from prison, but in II Timothy 4:16-18 we see Paul facing death calmly and even victoriously: "The Lord will deliver me from every evil work, and will save me unto his heavenly kingdom." He had indeed hoped that the Lord would come before his death, but he had never said that it would be so. In discussing marriage, he had once urged "the present distress" as a reason for remaining unmarried (I Cor. 7:26), and had said that "the time is shortened" (verse 29), language that by itself could mean that he felt the end to be very near. But if so, that was only a passing mood, and the language may refer rather to the troubled condition of the times. At any rate, what he here says must be interpreted in the light of his clear words elsewhere.

Paul lived in the conscious presence of the Lord

Jesus and hoped that Jesus might indeed come before he died, but he was gladly willing to wait and to labour on. "The night is far spent, the day is at hand: let us therefore cast off the works of darkness, and let us put on the armour of light" (Rom. 13:12). He had no patience with those who became fanatical on the subject of the Second Coming of Christ, as in Thessalonica, or with those who took no interest in this glorious hope. It was a constant spur with Paul to holy living and missionary activity. "For I am already being offered, and the time of my departure is come. I have fought the good fight, I have finished the course, I have kept the faith: henceforth there is laid up for me the crown of righteousness, which the Lord, the righteous judge, shall give to me at that day; and not to me only, but also to all them that have loved his appearing" (II Tim. 4:6-8). Death came to Paul before the Second Coming of Christ, but even so, he cherished the blessed hope of His coming. This is the attitude of the great hero of the Cross as he turns to meet the Master in death.

3. The Hope of All the Early Christians.

Paul was not alone in the buoyancy of this joyful hope. In I Corinthians 16:22, he gives in transliterated Greek an Aramaic prayer or watchword among the believers in Christ, *Marana tha* (our Lord, come). This rendering is in harmony with the language in Revelation 22:20, where Jesus "who testifieth these things" (cf. 1:2) says: "Yea, I come quickly," and

John replies joyfully: "Amen, come, Lord Jesus." This prayer reverberates throughout the New Testament from the time when the Lord was taken up from the sight of the disciples on Mount Olivet: "And while they were looking steadfastly into heaven as he went, behold two men stood by them in white apparel, who also said: Ye men of Galilee, why stand ye looking into heaven? this Jesus, who was received up from you into heaven, shall so come in like manner as ye beheld him going into heaven" (Acts 1:10 f.). This precious promise sustained the early disciples through all their many tribulations. Peter urges after Pentecost that the people turn again, that their sins may be blotted out, "so that there may come seasons of refreshing from the presence of the Lord; and that he may send the Christ who hath been appointed for you, even Jesus: whom the heaven must receive until the times of restoration of all things, whereof God spake by the mouth of his holy prophets that have been of old" (Acts 3:19-21). In one of the earliest, if not the very earliest, of the New Testament books, the Epistle of James (5:7), we read: "Be patient, therefore, until the coming of the Lord." In verse 8 the writer adds: "For the coming of the Lord is at hand."

They lived and laboured with a sense of the possible nearness of the Coming of the Lord. This they hoped for, but they planned and worked for the spread of the Kingdom as if the great event were millenniums away. Paul planned to conquer the Roman Empire for Christ, and did lay the foundation for that conquest. Peter in his Epistles refers to "the revelation of Jesus Christ" as a joyful anticipation. In the Apocalypse, John constantly pictures to the persecuted saints the coming of the victorious Christ, and urges confident enduring of all tribulations and trials with the certainty of the triumph of Christ in the end. The hope of the Second Coming of Christ was a powerful motive to holy living (II Pet. 3:11 f.), and to aggressive proclamation of the gospel message to men.

Chrysostom, indeed, interpreted *Marana tha* in I Corinthians 16:22 as meaning "Our Lord has come," and so of the Incarnation, not of the Second Coming. He uses the Incarnation thus as an appeal for holy living. *The Didache* (Teaching of the Twelve) uses *Marana tha* in the formula of invitation to the Lord's Supper. Paul, in his account of the institution of the Lord's Supper, reports Jesus as saying, "For as often as ye eat this bread, and drink the cup, ye proclaim the Lord's death till he come" (I Cor. 11:26). This ordinance thus points forward as well as looks backward. The fact that Paul gives *Marana tha* in the Aramaic probably means that the words "had become a sort of motto or password among Christians, and familiar in that shape, like 'Alleluia' with ourselves" (Robertson and Plummer). A like lively hope that the Lord is coming occurs in James 5:7 f; Philippians 4:5; Revelation 1:7. In Revelation 3:11, Jesus says,

"I come quickly," as in 22:20, though, to be sure, "quickly" has to be understood in terms of God's time, not ours. The early Christians lived in the tip-toe of expectancy and hope that Jesus would come soon, though they made no dogmatic statement to that effect.

4. The Promise of Jesus Himself.

This hope at bottom rests on what Jesus Himself said. In parabolic form the Master spoke of His Coming again and finding people unprepared, as they were in the days of Noah (Luke 17:26), and of Lot (verse 29). The apostles were puzzled over the sign of Christ's Coming again (Matt. 24:3), and asked Him about it on Olivet. In His reply Jesus spoke now of His death, now of the destruction of Jerusalem, and now of His Second Coming and the end of the world. We are not able to separate each item, but Jesus does speak of "the Son of man coming in clouds with great power and glory" (Mark 13:26). He adds various parables of warning to be ready for this Coming: "And what I say unto you, I say unto all, Watch" (Mark 13:37). Even before Caiaphas and the Sanhedrin, Jesus said, when asked whether He was the Christ, the Son of the Blessed (of God): "I am; and ye shall see the Son of man sitting at the right hand of power, and coming with the clouds of heaven." Caiaphas took it as blasphemy, but Jesus thus asserted His deity and foretold His Second Coming as King of glory. But the most definite and precious of all of Christ's promises concerning His Second Coming occurs in the Gospel of John, as in the Upper Room the Master consoled the disciples concerning His death. "And if I go and prepare a place for you, I come again, and will receive you unto myself; that where I am, there ye may be also. And whither I go, ye know the way" (John 14:3). Jesus comes for us at death, to be sure, and that is a blessed hope. But He is here speaking of His Second Coming and He gives us the most blessed picture of heaven that we have, that of being with Jesus and the Father, knowing them and our loved ones.

The Master promised to come back again. The Paraclete takes the place of Christ meanwhile here on earth; in fact, through the Holy Spirit, Jesus is with us always, even unto the end of the world (Matt. 28:20). The Holy Spirit is the supreme Teacher of Christ, and takes of the things of Christ and makes them ours. But even so, Christ Himself will come again to proclaim His victory over sin, and for salvation to them that wait for Him (Heb. 9:27 f.). Jesus foretold Peter's death and urged him, "Follow me." Peter had instinctive curiosity about John, and could not refrain from asking: "And what shall this man do?" Instantly, the Master answered: "If I will that he tarry till I come, what is that to thee? Follow thou me" (John 21:21 f.). This was after His resurrection and Jesus thus pointedly again foretold His personal return to earth. But He did not say that John would live on till that great event. "This saying therefore went forth among the brethren, that that disciple should not die," yet Jesus did not say it. The aged John did live longer than any of the apostles and, as he was writing at the end of the century, he took pains to correct this misunderstanding of the words of Jesus to Peter. John met death in his old age, still looking for the Second Coming of Christ, whom he had served and loved so long.

5. This Hope Calls for Holy Living by Us.

This is the very point in Titus 2:12-14. Certainly there is no ground for disbelief or for impatience. Times are not for us to know on this subject, Paul taught. Peter insisted that God's clock is not our clock. When Jesus says "quickly" or "soon," we must bear this in mind. The essential thing for us is to know and to believe that Jesus will come again in person. He expressly said that only the Father knew the time. How idle it is, therefore, for men to set dates for that Coming and to work out elaborate schemes and charts about it. The point that concerns each one of us is to be ready for His Coming, to live a holy life, "looking for and hastening the coming of the day of God" (II Pet. 3:12). "Our citizenship is in heaven; whence also we wait for a Saviour, the Lord Jesus Christ" (Phil. 3:20). We look for Him eagerly and joyfully. He will come in His own good time. We may go to Him by death before He comes again to earth. That is immaterial, if our heart is right toward

Him and our faces are set toward Him. If we live to share in His glorious Coming, we shall be happy, "whether at even, or at cockcrowing, or in the morning" (Mark 13:35). Meanwhile, "in the now time" we should lead pious, holy, righteous lives, brightened and chastened by this blessed hope in Christ, purifying ourselves even as He is pure.

XII

PAUL'S PRAYER FOR THE EPHESIANS

"For this reason I bow my knees to the Father, from whom every family in heaven and on earth is named, that he would grant you, according to the riches of his glory, to be strengthened with power through his Spirit in the inward man; that Christ may dwell in your hearts through faith; that ye, rooted and grounded in love, may get strength to comprehend together with all the saints what is the breadth and length and height and depth, and to know the love of Christ that surpasses knowledge; that ye may be filled unto all the fulness of God."—EPHESIANS 3:14-21.

THIS marvellous prayer is really the second in this Epistle, the first one being 1:15-23. It is probably a circular letter to the churches in the province of Asia, including Ephesus, and is apparently the same as the one to Laodicea, mentioned in Colossians 4:16. If so, these two prayers were not merely for the church in Ephesus, though Paul has them in mind. The prayers of Paul are remarkable for their variety, their pungency, their pertinence, their power. Prayer is one index of the man's character, if he really prays as Paul does, for definite mercies and blessings. As a rule, public prayer is the poorest performance in public worship, poorer than the singing or the sermon, which are often poor enough. Paul's prayers are not platitudinous nor pious generalities. He does not, like the Pharisees, pray to be heard of men. His prayers are not like that reported as the most eloquent prayer ever addressed to a Boston audience. We are concerned with this greatest of Paul's prayers, for nowhere else does he sound such depths or reach such heights of spiritual emotion as here. The first prayer (1:15-23) is about God's redemptive purpose, while this overflows with the wealth of God's love, like John 3:16. It is an interrupted prayer, begun in 3:1 and resumed in 3:14. Calvin thinks that Paul actually bent his knees as he dictated this prayer, but that is not necessary. Both kneeling and standing are common attitudes in prayer in the New Testament, and in Gethsemane Jesus was prone upon His face in His agony. There are four petitions in this prayer.

1. For Strength in the Inward Man.

Paul is fond of the distinction between the inward man and the outward man. Strength in the outward man is not to be despised. The ancients took pride in athletic exercises and prizes. Health of body and strength of muscle are good as far as they go. But one may be strong, like Samson, in muscular prowess and weak, like Samson, in temptation. Who is the strong man? The elephant and the lion can be overcome by the skill of man. The winner of the prize fight may fail to stand in the battle of Mansoul, which every man has to wage. The real battle of life is the inward struggle. This is where the victory is won or lost. As a man thinks in his heart, so is he. Out of the heart are the issues of life. The outward man may perish, as it will, while the inward man is renewed day by day (II Cor. 4:16) and wins in the end. One may have the form of godliness and deny the power thereof. This inward man Paul calls the "new man," renewed according to the image of Christ (Col. 3:10).

Many a man with a fine reputation has a sudden fall. He may have been a preacher, a deacon, a bank president, a trusted official. He has been leading a double life and was not sound within, like a great oak, rotten in the heart, that crashes before a sudden storm. The only way to get this inward strength is through the Holy Spirit, who takes hold of our weakness and gives us strength to withstand the tempter's blows. Some of the old monks painted Mary on the outside of the convents and Venus on the inside. But the Spirit cleanses the inner man, according to the riches of God's glory, abundant resources for us all. This is the paradox of the Christian life, as Paul said: "When I am weak, then am I strong." For then we look to and lean on Christ. "I am able to do all things in the one who keeps on empowering me." He strengthens us with power, and the strength abides as we abide in Him. God wants reality and looks beyond the profession to the impression.

2. For Christ in the Heart.

"That Christ may dwell in your hearts through faith." This petition is closely related to the preceding. That is a plea for strength in the inward man through the Holy Spirit; this for the indwelling of Christ, the Son of God, in the heart. We need Christ in this inward struggle with sin. He has promised to be with us all the days, and we need His presence all the time. Paul's prayer here is that we will let Christ make His home in our hearts. There are some people that we are glad to see in an occasional visit, whom we should greatly dislike to make their home with us. Are we quite sure that we wish Christ to make His home in our hearts, to know all the secrets hidden there? If we let Him come in to rule over us, we must give Him all the keys to every room, to every closet, every drawer. That may be inconvenient, but it is inevitable. And then the one with whom we have to do knows all the thoughts and intents of the heart. They are all laid bare to His eye. He is our spiritual surgeon and sees it all. This is a mystery, to be sure, a blessed mystery, but not impossible.

Jesus stands at the door of every heart, knocking for permission to enter. "If any one hear my voice and open the door, I shall come in to him and shall sup with him and he with me." Let Him in as a guest, then as Master and Lord, then as Friend and Elder Brother. Thus you will have fellowship, even here, that is a foretaste of heaven on earth, the promise of the life that now is and that is to be. Jesus will not stay in any heart in this high fellowship without trust. He comes in at the call of faith and He remains on the same terms of perfect confidence. Try Christ on that basis. "If any one love me, he will keep my word; and the Father will love him, and we shall come unto him, and make our abode with him" (John 14:23). Are you willing to accept this challenge of Christ? Do you wish the Father and the Son to make their "abode" with you? Let Christ "dwell in your heart by faith," and it will be done. One thing is certain, that if Christ comes in, there will be a first-class house-cleaning before you let Him in, and the house will stay cleaner. Some former visitors will not be welcome any more. The Unseen Guest will make a difference in the life of the home. It may come to pass with you, as with Paul: "For me living is Christ and dying is gain." Christ will cover the circumference of your life. He will encompass it all. It will be Christ's home, so that no longer do you live to yourself, but Christ lives in you, the hope of glory, the joy of life.

3. For Comprehension of the Love of Christ.

Christ's love for us, I take Paul to mean, as he said in II Corinthians 5:14: "For the love of Christ holds us together." So Paul prays that the Ephesians may gain some grasp of the breadth, length, height, and depth of Christ's love for them; what Alexander

Maclaren called "the rectangular measure of Christ's love." It is as long as eternity into the eternal purpose of the Father and Son to redeem men. It is as broad and wide as human need, and leaps over all barriers of race, age, sex, class, rank, and station. It is deep as human sin, and can touch the lost and loveless. It is as high as heaven itself, and comes out of the very heart of God who is love, and Christ is God's love incarnate. And yet it is futile to try to measure the measureless love of Christ, the paradox of all paradoxes, beyond all comprehension. God so loved the world that He gave His own Son, the best gift He had. "O the depth of the riches both of the knowledge and the wisdom of God," the love that passes all knowledge. And yet Paul prays that the Ephesians may come to know something of it. This is only possible if they themselves are "rooted and grounded in love." This is the probable way to take the phrase "in love," and it is an obvious truth, one without love can form no conception of Christ's love for sinners. But a mother who risks, and sometimes gives, her life for her child can get a glimmering of this surpassing love of Christ. She can know the unknowable. The sceptic, the infidel, is ruled out of court on this question of God's love. "I know him whom I have believed." I know Him, even if you do not. The love of Christ is not settled by cold intellectuals, agnostics, ignoramuses on this subject. The mother knows what love is.

As a matter of fact, every real Christian knows. It is a universal brotherhood and fellowship, "together with all the saints." All round the world through all the ages the elect of God have let Christ come into their hearts, and under the guidance of the Holy Spirit they have caught glimpses—precious moments—of the wonders of Christ's love for sinners. Two men on board a ship could not understand each other's language. They saw each other reading the New Testament. One said, "Amen." The other said, "Hallelujah." They embraced each other in Christ. They had the fellowship of the saints, the common bond in Christ Jesus. They had experience with Christ, the best of all knowledge, "the knowledge of Jesus, the most excellent of the sciences."

4. For the Fulness of God.

"That ye may be filled unto all the fulness of God." One almost hesitates to pray a prayer like this, so daring does it seem. And yet we know that Paul does not mean that we are to become equal to God, but only kin to God in nature and life. Peter has spoken of our having become partakers of the divine nature (II Pet. 1:4). This is what John means by the new birth (John 3:3; 5:1). It is Paul's own idea in Romans 8:29: "Because whom he did foreknow, he foreordained, to be conformed to the image of his Son, that he should be the first-born among many brethren." And Jesus Himself set before us the goal of perfection: "Ye shall therefore be perfect as your heavenly Father is perfect" (Matt. 5:48). Likeness to Christ is the glorious destiny of the saints, washed in His blood and changed into His image. We do not yet know how glorious that will be, nor precisely what we shall be, only this, that if He is manifested, we shall be like Him, for we shall see Him as He is (I John 3:2). That is glory enough to fascinate any one.

Paul seems to realize that this climax in his prayer may stagger the faith of some. So in his doxology he hastens to assure his readers that he has not overreached the love or the power of God. Our God is able to do all that Paul here asks or that we can conceive. He is able to do above all our highest dreams, yea, abundantly above it all, piling Pelion on Ossa, in the greatness of His plans for us. He has the power, and we need not long for too little in our spiritual growth in Christ. As for himself, Paul was never content with the new knowledge gained of Christ, who led him like a flying goal, always in sight and yet always advancing, this upward goal that lures us on to God. Some day we shall know even as we are known. We shall see Christ face to face in the fulness of His beauty. Perfect love casts out fear here, and only perfect love can exist with Christ. Thus there will be glory in the Church, the Bride of Christ, and in Christ Himself through all the ages.

Paul has asked for much in this noble prayer: for strength through the Holy Spirit, for the dwelling of

Christ in the heart, for richer knowledge of Christ's love for us, for ultimate likeness to the Father, for the touch of each person of the Trinity in our lives. But he has not asked for too much. He is not thinking of a gusher that soon runs dry, but of a ceaseless flow of the oil of God's grace in our lives that enriches our souls forever. In this prayer Paul prays for the essentials in the Christian life, without which there can be no eternal life. He has in it the great doctrines of grace, but far more than creed. There is here the contact of the spirit of man with God, of God with man, of transformation of heart and life by God's Spirit, of lofty communion with Christ, of final entrance into the family of the Father in heaven.

Let us pray this prayer in moments when we are down and things look dark. Lift up your eyes to the hills and catch this glimpse of the glory of God even here, as its radiance shines all about us. Over in Geneva I once saw a strange brilliance on everything after sundown. It was the Alpine afterglow from Mont Blanc. That lofty peak caught the glory of the setting sun, long after it was no longer visible elsewhere, and threw it back upon Geneva. Paul has taken us into the very presence of God in this prayer. We can enter again into this holy of holies.

XIII

THE BLESSINGS OF JUSTIFICATION BY FAITH

"Having therefore been justified by faith, let us enjoy peace with God through our Lord Jesus Christ."—ROMANS 5:1.

IN the previous part of Romans, Paul has shown the *need* of justification by both Gentile and Jew (1:18–3:16); the *nature* of justification (being set right with God), as God's own plan of grace in the propitiatory death of His Son, appropriated by faith on our part (3:21-31); and has given a striking *illustration* of faith in the case of Abraham before he was circumcised (4). He has yet to discuss the *result* of justification, that is, sanctification (6-8). Both justification (an act) and sanctification (a process) are included in Paul's doctrine of the God-kind of righteousness, which is the theme of this greatest of his Epistles (1:14-17). He pauses here to look at the blessings assured to the individual who is set right with God (5:1-11).

1. Justification Assumed as a Glorious Fact.

"Having therefore been justified by faith." This fact lies behind what he has further to say. He has already made full and fair discussion of the way by which we are reconciled to God. "We received the reconciliation" through Jesus Christ (5:11). It is God's overture to the sinner. God's own plan of redemption for man through the gift of His own Son, as a propitiation for sin, has enabled God to justify the sinner and remain just Himself as He has to do (3:23-25). An effort has been made to explain away the plain meaning of this language concerning the atoning death of Christ, because some theologians have difficulty in making a reasonable and satisfactory theory of the atonement. The new psychology cannot get rid of sin. But this is God's problem, not ours. It is entirely possible that even theologians are not quite equal to the task of comprehending and explaining this problem. Substitution is clearly in it. Christ died for us, and in our stead became sin for us, and suffered for us. But substitution by no means exhausts all the meaning of the death of Christ. There is more in it of mystery and of love and of grace than all our theories can discover.

The revolt against the death of Christ, as the basis for our justification through faith, is due largely to a lessened sense of sin on the part of modern men. It was the weight of the sin of the world that broke the heart of Christ on the Cross. Paul saw it clearly when he says that God "made him to be sin who did not know sin" (II Cor. 5:21). Even Jesus did not know beforehand how terrible it would be to be so regarded by the Father, who left Him with a sense of desolation as He bore it. But beyond our comprehension as it all is, it was done "that we might become the righteousness of God in him." Hence Paul pleads for reconciliation with God as Christ's ambassador to men. This glorious fact lies at the basis of Paul's theology. There is no other hope for man outside of the Cross of Christ. "There is therefore now no condemnation to those in Christ Jesus" (8:1).

2. Enjoyment of Peace with God Now Possible.

"Let us enjoy peace with God through our Lord Jesus Christ." The King James and the American Standard translation are from the *Textus Receptus,* which is based on late manuscripts: "We have peace with God." This is not the correct text and, if correct, would be tautological, a mere restatement of "having been justified by faith." All the old Greek manuscripts have the present subjunctive, *echōmen,* not the present indicative *echomen.* It is the volitive or hortatory use of the subjunctive, and the action is linear, not punctiliar. The rendering, "Let us have peace," sounds as if Paul meant, "Let us make peace." But the ingressive aorist subjunctive, *schōmen eirēnēn,* would be required for that idea. Paul used this ingressive aorist subjunctive, *schō,* in Romans 1:13: "that I may get some fruit among you also." We have it also in Matthew 21:38. Here the linear present can only mean, "Let us go on having (enjoying) peace," precisely as the imperfect indicative is used in

Acts 9:31, where we read that, after Saul's conversion, the church "enjoyed peace" (*eichen eirēnēn*). The exhortation, as Paul wrote it and meant it, is entirely pertinent. It is not a mere logical and doctrinal complacency that Paul has in mind, but the full enjoyment of the blessed inheritance that the believer has as a child of God. Vincent, in his *Word Studies,* insists that the subjunctive here makes no sense, and even Thayer says that "we must read" the indicative. Homer can nod and great scholars can, and often do, fail to see the meaning of a Greek tense. Theirs is then the nonsense, not Paul's.

Peace has already been made through Christ, "through whom we have had our introduction into this grace in which we stand." We have been presented at court by Christ. We are on acceptable terms in Christ with our heavenly Father. It is now our privilege and duty to come boldly to the throne of grace and obtain help in every time of need. Hambone, that shrewd Memphis philosopher of negro wit, says: "My old woman got all the religion she's going to get. What she now needs is to cultivate what she's got." There is a type of introspective religion that leads to a static stage of inactivity and doubt, to lurking doubt that paralyzes faith. Doubt your doubts and put your faith to the test. God is still in His heaven, as Browning's Pippa says, and all is well with the world.

All will be well with us if we go on enjoying peace with God and with men. It may not be possible always to live in peace with some men, but our own skirts should be clean. "If possible, live in peace with all men, so far as in you lies" (Rom. 12:18). If all Christians lived up to this rule of life in private and public affairs, the world would be a happier place to live in and war would die of starvation. There was an old woman who said that she was never so happy as when she was miserable, and the dear old saint paraded her mournful piety on all occasions. Christians themselves, by the multitude of their complainings, have given so-called Christian Science an opportunity to put emphasis on cheerfulness. Joy should be the dominant note in every Christian's life. He should not need to sing: "Where is the blessedness I knew when first I saw the Lord?" He should have more joy now than then.

3. And Glorying in Hope of the Glory of God.

"And let us keep on glorying on the basis of the glory of God." Wonderful as the present peace of heart is, since we have been justified by faith, there is greater glory to come. The golden age of the ancients was in the past, but Christianity points ahead. There are better days on earth and far greater ones in heaven. The old preachers may have put too much emphasis on the bliss of heaven, but certainly most preachers today have too little to say about it. In fact, some of them do not even believe in a future life at all, if we can believe a recent questionnaire sent out to the Detroit pastors. Such ministers see only the life that now is and discuss simply the social problems of the day, and there are plenty of them in all conscience—problems of labour, of capital, of money, of poverty, of proper housing, of the slums, of unemployment, of education, of race hatred, of the newspapers, of the movies, of the radio, of the underworld, of the gangsters, of liquor, of the politicians. But these problems are not religion, though we do need religion before we are willing or able to handle them.

Some of the modern reformers have dropped spiritual religion entirely and adopt humanism or behaviourism or psychoanalysis or communism, or some other fad as the panacea for human ills. But they do not cure any more than the cure-alls of other quacks. Some look on man as a mere animal, and one of them talks about "the myth of the soul." Certainly he has a very small one. Recently *The Wall Street Journal*, which cannot be accused of being a theological paper, said that the greatest need of the United States in its conflict with crime was belief in God and in immortality. If we have faith in God, we have hope for the present and the future. Otherwise we are like the heathen, "having no hope and without God in the world" (Eph. 2:12). The Christian is an optimist with the only ground for true optimism, God. The godless man is necessarily a pessimist or a sensualist.

4. And Glorying in Tribulations Also.

"But let us also keep on glorying in tribulations." There are those who are loud in expressions of praise to God so long as they prosper. The devil challenged Job's piety, but Job lost all and still said: "Though he slay me, yet will I trust him." This he said after his miserable comforters had turned against him and his own wife suggested that he curse God and die. It is not so hard to preach joy in tribulations to other people, but it is not easy to sing for joy when the blows fall on one's own head. The word tribulation is from the Latin *tribulum,* the threshing flail used to beat out the grain from the straw. The Greek word *thlipsis* means pressure like a rock on the chest. The Stoics took trouble heroically until the burden was too heavy, and then turned to suicide as the way out, as too many unbalanced people, alas, do today. The Christian hero endures to the end, and finds joy in Christ in the midst of the troubles that overwhelm him.

Paul does not urge that we rejoice because of tribulations. God can bring good to us out of trouble. That is often His way. But we are to trust God and go on with a song in our heart and a smile on our face, even if the tears rain down at the same time. The Epicurean tried to drown trouble in pleasure and dissipation, like those today who turn to drink or to sensual pleasures in order to forget their trouble. But this is the lowest plane of life. Tennyson sang of "broken purposes" that strike us hard, but by and by these very disappointments can become stepping-stones to power and service. Christ stooped to conquer sin.

Paul gives a chain of evidence for his exhortation to glory in tribulations, "knowing," he says. It is like the links in a chain or the successive growths each year in the tree. The first reason given is that "tribulation works patience." We greatly need patience, endurance, or remaining under without complaining about the load. But we are not born with this spirit of adjustment, and we gain it by experience, by the test of tribulations. On the River Rhine there grows a flower with a supple stem that allows the blossom to rest on the water at high tide or low tide. Then "patience works experience." When trouble comes again, we treat it as an old acquaintance. We turn to God for help as we did before. When David met Goliath, he was not afraid. He had met a lion and a bear, and God had delivered him. Then he is not afraid even of Goliath. We are often cowards in the present crisis because we have not had experience with God in former trials. If the Son of God has walked with us in the furnace, we do not fear the fiery trials that now rage round us. And "experience works hope." We come to expect God to be our ever present help in trouble. Wherefore we are not afraid. The lapidaries on the coast of Wales have learned that the most precious stones are swept up in the worst storms. Hope means to open the eyes. Experience opens the eyes so that we see the hand of God when others do not. We see the rainbow in the rain and we know that we shall not be put to shame. This is experimental religion, putting God to the test, one of the supreme blessings of justification by faith.

5. And We Have the Supreme Proof of God's Love in Christ.

"God's love has been poured out in our hearts through the Holy Spirit who has been given to us" (5:5). In our hearts the Holy Spirit has given us the rich and priceless experiences of God's love, as shown in the gift of His Son. "While we were yet weak, in due time Christ died for the ungodly." God commends His unbounded love to us "because, while we were yet sinners Christ died for us." That is the heart of the whole matter. What sort of a heart has a man who will not respond to love like that? It is the Father's loving plan, the soul's glad offering of himself, the Holy Spirit's tender and powerful pleading with us. Paul is not afraid of the blood of Christ, as some modern sentimental humanitarians are. We were justified by the blood of Christ, Paul bluntly says (5:9), and we shall reach final salvation by the life of Christ, who ever lives to intercede for us. Christ has not given up the work of redemption. He died for us; He rose from the grave; He ascended on high to the right hand of the Father; there as our High Priest He is our Advocate, while the Holy Spirit is the Advocate with us on earth. What more can even God do for us than He has done? Having been reconciled with God by Christ, "let us glory in God through our Lord Jesus Christ."

Paul pleads for an exultant faith, for a triumphant faith, for a conquering faith. "Faith is the victory that overcomes the world," John says, and it is. Marshal Foch said that an army is never whipped till the general thinks that it is. Then hope is gone. So up and at the hosts of sin. Christ will win. Let us not betray Him anywhere at any time. Let us have a jubilant faith that will sweep back the forces of Satan. It can be done. It will be done, when and if we look to the Master and follow Him all the way, even to the Cross.

XIV

LOYALTY TO JESUS

"Let us therefore go on out to him without the camp, bearing his reproach."—HEBREWS 13:13.

THE Epistle to the Hebrews is a powerful and passionate plea to the Jewish Christians not to desert Christianity for Judaism, as they were tempted to do by their Jewish friends. These Jewish neighbours argued that the Jewish religion was superior to Christianity because of the prophets who preached it, the angels who were associated with its origin, Moses who gave the law, the Aaronic priesthood which gave glory to it. The author meets the challenge boldly, and overwhelmingly shows that Christianity is superior to Judaism because of Jesus, the very one who was the "stumbling-block" to them, the "crucified criminal"—nay, the Risen Messiah, the Son of God, the Lord of Glory. He does not mince matters in the least. He is not ashamed of the human name Jesus, but that name tells only part of the story. As the Son of God Jesus is superior to the Old Testament prophets (1:1-3), to the angels (1:4–2:18), both in His deity and in His humanity (because in the Incarnation He rises above angels in His human nature), to Moses (3:1–4:13), to the whole Levitical priesthood (4:16–12:3). In all the great argument, the greatest apologetic for Christianity in existence, the author warns the readers against apostasy as a hopeless performance, and challenges them to be true to the faith which they professed. In the passage before us in this sermon (13:7-17), he makes one last eloquent plea for loyalty to Jesus, Himself, because of what He is, what He has done for us, and what He will do for us. This is the logical climax that drives home the entire prolonged and sustained appeal.

1. Jesus Suffered Without the Gate.

The Old Testament gives the ritual for the offering of animal sacrifices (Lev. 4:12 f, 21; 16:27; Ex. 29: 14; 32:26 f); and that is restated here in verse 11: "The bodies of those animals whose blood is brought into the holy place by the high priest are burned without the camp." The parallel with the example of Jesus is complete. He is the better sacrifice that Christianity has (9:13–10:18), that does make eternal redemption and cleanse the conscience from sin. "Jesus also, that he might sanctify the people by his own blood, suffered without the gate of the city" (answering to the camp in Leviticus). The writer is not afraid or ashamed of the blood of Christ. The rather he glories in it. The life is in the blood, and Jesus gave that for us on Golgotha's hill, "the place of the skull" that looks like a skull. He is the Lamb of God, slain outside the city's walls. Jesus bore His own cross on the way till relieved by Simon of Cyrene at the command of the soldiers, and He went all the way to Calvary, "despising the shame of the Cross," and died upon it.

This is the central fact about Jesus Christ, the Son of God and Son of man, that is here presented to the Jewish Christians as the final and conclusive reason for loyalty to Him. It matters little whether we comprehend at all the mystery of the Cross whereon Jesus suffered and died, and whereon our own sins were nailed, so that in a real though mystical sense, as Paul says, we were crucified with Christ. There is the supreme fact of Christianity, the death of Christ on the Cross for our sins. Let preachers who will omit the cross from their sermons; they thereby change Christianity to a system of ethics. Some tender sentimentalists even revolt at the blood of Christ in our hymns. Not such was the writer of Hebrews, or Paul, or John, or Peter, or Christ Himself.

2. Jesus Calls Us to Come to His Side.

"Let us therefore go on to him without the camp, bearing his reproach." This is the plea of the writer. It is a manly plea that any soldier can understand when his captain leads the way into danger. Instead of giving up Christ and going back to Judaism, if a cleavage has to come, give up Judaism and go out and take your stand with Christ outside the gate, beyond the pale of the old Judaism. Come on "over the top" to Christ on Calvary. Show your colours for Christ. It is a plea for frank declaration about Christ. The war is on, and "no man's land" is no place for a follower of Christ, where one is shot at from both sides. The so-called secret disciples should be ashamed of themselves, like those Pharisees who believed in Jesus and yet did not confess Him, because they cared more for the praise of men (their fellow Pharisees) than the praise of God. Jesus constantly said, "Follow me!" All right, then; follow Christ to His Cross, and bear whatever reproach may come for doing so. Let men ridicule you as behind the times, if they wish to do so. They rejected Christ before they did you. The slave is not greater than his Master. Do it now. Tomorrow may be too late. Nicodemus and Joseph of Arimathea put off confession of Christ till He had died. Then they came out into the open. Better late than never. But they missed the joy of letting Jesus see them line up with Him while He was alive.

There is nothing more needed today all over the world than open and courageous championship of Jesus Christ, as Redeemer and Lord. If I had only one word to say to the young men and women of this generation (the old are usually too far gone for hope), it would be to heed the call of Christ to come out by His side, to join the cause of Christ under Him as the Captain and Perfecter of faith, the Conqueror of evil and wrong among men. Taking such a stand with Christ at once ennobles any life, enriches any heart, opens a horizon of boundless scope, girds one with power to attempt the highest things for God and man.

3. Have Courage to Break Away from the Slackers.

The Jewish friends clamoured for return to the faith of the fathers, without the new-fangled twist given to it by Paul, who actually claimed that Christianity is the true Judaism. There is always a tremendous pull in one's set or group. Boys go with the gang, girls with their circle or set. It requires courage to step out alone from the group with which one has run. This was true of Gentile Christians as well as Jewish Christians. The old Gentile comrades thought it strange that the new Christians no longer ran with their old habits of revelling, carousing, excesses, idolatries. Today young Christians are jeered at by some if they do not drink, and if they attend church Sunday night in preference to the movies. But we are not saved by the wholesale. One by one we volunteer into the service of Christ, volunteer even if no one else does, even because no one else does, for then Christ needs us more.

Loyalty is a great word, one of the noblest in the language, as Dr. J. A. Hutton rightly holds in his fine book, *Loyalty, the Approach to Faith.* The brave soldier will fight on alone, like Alvin York, and "one put ten thousand to flight." There are some who can muster up courage to die for Christ who are not brave enough to live for Him day by day in the midst of condescension, ridicule, social boycott. Patriotism is heroic, but piety in an unfavourable environment calls for the highest courage, especially if we are surrounded by slackers, deserters. Dependability is a fine trait in any character. Without it there is little left that is worth while in life. Can Christ count on you to be true to Him, whatever others do or do not do; and everywhere, even in the midst of those who do not love Him? Social ostracism cuts deep into one's feelings, but the disciple of Christ has to be ready to receive the cut direct from former companions who passed as friends. They will accuse you of putting on airs, of posing as superior, finally of being hypocrites. The example of Paul is at hand, when he returned from Damascus to Jerusalem. He had gone out the chief persecutor of Christians. On his return as a Christian he was the scorn of the Sanhedrin who had sent him out, now a turncoat and a renegade Jew. He was also under suspicion by the disciples whom he had been persecuting, who were unable to see how the fierce wolf that ravined the fold could now be a lamb within the fold. It was not till Barnabas championed the new convert that he had any friends. Then Peter took him home with him and they had rare fellowship together. When Jesus hung on the Cross, some of those who scoffed at Him had hailed Him as the Messiah of Israel on the preceding Sunday morning as He rode into Jerusalem. The enemies of Christ (the Sanhedrin) first mocked Him, and the soldiers took it up, and even the two robbers at first, though one repented.

4. And Stand by the Leaders for Christ.

Loyalty to Christ involves loyalty to those who are loyal to Him. This is specially exhorted here: "Remember your leaders who spoke to you the word of God" (Heb. 13:7). The church in Jerusalem had had great leaders, the apostles Peter and John in particular. Stephen was the first martyr for Christ, and he had been followed by James the brother of John. But they should not forget Barnabas and James the Lord's brother. They must imitate the faith of such noble leaders. It is impossible to exaggerate the influence of great leaders of the past who have followed Christ to the end, a glorious heritage to the Church. But the present leaders also are to be obeyed as they lead us on towards Christ. It is treason when a leader, like Benedict Arnold, goes over to the other side. That does sometimes happen. Judas is the outstanding example of treachery to Christ. Sometimes leaders put their ears to the ground, as Aaron did when Moses was on the Mount, to listen to the murmur of the groundlings.

The writer of Hebrews has in mind (13:7) only leaders who really follow Christ and lead all who will rally to His cause. Such pastors are sleepless over the report that they will have to render for each one under their leadership, "that they may do it with joy and not groaning, for this is not advantageous to you." There will be a roll-call by and by, and the truth about each one will have to be told. If the pastor's hands are upheld and not hindered, the work will prosper. It is amazing in any large church, how many members simply disappear, drop out of the ranks.

5. Thus You Will Share the Victory with Christ. He endured the Cross, and won the crown. He despised the shame of death on the Cross, rose from the dead and has taken His seat at the right hand of the throne of God. He calls upon us to bear each his own cross, as we find it in our path of service. No cross, no crown. We do not have to make an offering for sin. Christ did that once for all. The Roman Catholics are wrong in looking on the mass as a repetition of the sacrifice of Christ on Calvary. He does not have to repeat that supreme and final offering. But we are called on to render to God spiritual sacrifices of praise and service, the fruit of the lips and the obedience of the heart, well-doing and liberality. With such offerings God is well-pleased.

Why should they wish to desert Christ? He has not changed: "Jesus Christ yesterday and today the same and for the ages." There is no room for a new Christ, a modern Christ, a Nordic Christ. There is only one Christ, the Saviour of the world. He is sufficient for all who will believe in Him and take Him as Lord and Redeemer. He alone is the hope of the world. Paul gloried in the Cross of Christ as alone worth while (Gal. 6:14). Men change, with their fancies and their fads, but Christ is universal, the Son of mankind. He is exhaustless. No new thought can surpass Him. He can never be a mere "landmark," as a noted professor suggested in a review article. He is always the goal ahead of us, calling us to high thinking and noble living. No system of ethics has ever reached the Sermon on the Mount. No human life has ever matched the earthly life of Jesus. And yet He is not beyond our hope. He is our Elder Brother, and always understands and helps those who are willing to have Him rule in their hearts. Others may be disloyal, but not Jesus. Confess Him before men, and He will confess you in heaven.

XV

HEAVEN AS HOME

"For we know that if our earthly house of this tabernacle be dissolved, we have a building from God, a house not made with hands, eternal in the heavens."—II CORINTHIANS 5:1.

WE use heaven in the sense of sky, and also as the abode of God and the redeemed. The Greek word *ouranos* is also employed in both senses. We are not here concerned with theories about the location of heaven, as the place where the blessed in Christ dwell. We know that God is spirit and that it is the redeemed spirit of man, not the body of flesh and blood, that enters heaven in this sense. The resurrection body is a spiritual body, linked in some wonderful way with the earthly body, but different and infinitely more glorious. The New Testament knows nothing of an intermediate state, by any name whatever. Death is the portal at which all enter their final abode, which is confirmed at the general judgment. The language in the New Testament about heaven is, of course, figurative and symbolic, and must be so understood. Only we know that the reality far surpasses the wonderful pictures given us.

There are some clear statements made that should cheer all believers in Christ, as they face the close of the earthly life. Jesus has robbed the grave of its victory and of its terror. By His own death and resurrection He has overthrown the devil's power, and there is no more ground for fear (Heb. 2:14 f). And He has given us the picture of heaven as home, that brightens the New Testament and gives us a rainbow of hope far beyond the will-o-the-wisps of spiritualism. Jesus is the one qualified to tell us what we need to know, because He came from the Father and went back to Him. He begs us to trust Him on this very point (John 14:1). The New Testament everywhere confirms the words of Jesus about heaven.

1. Here We Are Strangers and Pilgrims.

The classic passage is Hebrews 11:13-16. Just as Abraham left his home in Ur of the Chaldees and went forth, "not knowing where he was going" (Heb. 11:8), dwelt in tents (tabernacles) with Isaac and Jacob, looking for the city whose builder and maker is God, and died without having seen the Messiah come, so we are "strangers and pilgrims upon the earth," "seeking for our fatherland," which is heaven. Earth is not our real, our permanent home. This does not mean that the Christian is not to take seriously his life here on earth, that he is to be aloof from his responsibilities and duties as a citizen, and to admit without a contest the devil's claim to ownership of the life of the world. There is ample proof, in lawlessness of all kinds and in rampant excesses of sin, that the world still lies in the grip of the evil one. But the Master refused compromise with Satan and chose warfare with him, and calls us to like contest against sin. We are to be in the world, but not of it—a lesson for all Christians to learn. Our real citizenship is in heaven, as Paul says. We are therefore a colony of heaven here on earth. Each group of Christians is a sample of heaven, to show men what that community ought to be, to make it a fit place for citizens of heaven to live in. Peter likewise looks on Christians as "sojourners" on earth (I Pet. 1:1, 17; 2:11), for a while till we go on home.

2. Meanwhile We Are Dwelling in a Tent with the Title Deed to Our Permanent Home.

In II Corinthians 5:1-9, Paul gives a graphic contrast between the body as a tent, "our earthly house of the tabernacle," and, "the building from God, a house not made with hands, eternal, in the heavens." The tent is useful and necessary, and this very word is used of heaven as the prototype (the heavenly tabernacle) of the one commanded for Moses to build, after which the temple was copied. The word also is used of the dwelling of God with men (Rev. 21:3). The body as a tent is not to be despised or mistreated. The rather, as the present home of the soul, it is the temple of God (I Cor. 3:17), and hence is sacred to God and not for the devil's use (I Cor. 6:19). But after all, this tent has inevitable limitations, in spite of its wonderful capabilities and powers, and we often "groan" in it and because of it (II Cor. 5:4). While we are "at home in the body" in a real sense, "we are away from the Lord" (5:4) in the full sense. So then, Paul does not desire to live on forever in this tent. He longs the rather to be present with the Lord in the complete sense. "For to me living is Christ and dying is gain" (Phil. 1:21). But Paul feels that he already has while in the body the title to the heavenly home: "We have a building from God." This blessed fact is made plain by Hebrews 11:1, where the word *hypostasis* (basis, foundation, title-deed in the papyri) is used of faith: "Now faith is the title-deed of things hoped for, the proof of things not seen." We have here and now the title-deed to the home in heaven. We shall enter it by and by and present our title-deed for occupancy, even the word of Jesus Christ, who purchased it for us by His own blood (I Pet. 1:18 f.; Rev. 5:6, 9; 7:14).

3. We Have the Promise of Jesus to Take Us Home.

We have it in the most precious picture of heaven found anywhere, in John 14:1-7. Jesus is speaking to the distressed and puzzled disciples about His own approaching death and their reunion with Him. He had just said, that where He was going they could not follow just now, much to the disturbance of boastful and self-confident Simon Peter (John 13:36-38). Now he bids their hearts cease their fluttering of anxiety, and appeals for trust in Him such as they have in God the Father. Then the Master added: "In my Father's house (home) are many abiding-places," using the same word (*monē*) as in verse 25, of the Father and the Son dwelling with the believer: "We shall come to him and make our abode with him."

The language is not to be taken physically of an actual house, any more than the picture of heaven as foursquare in Revelation 21 is to be so interpreted. It is not a spatial picture of heaven as an enormous apartment house, but of heaven as home, with God as the central figure in it and with room in God's heart and home for each of us. Luther Burbank pathetically renounced belief in heaven because there were so many souls that heaven could not contain them. What a tragic literalistic misinterpretation of the words of Jesus! The materialism of the nineteenth century (of Huxley, for instance) still obscures and beclouds many minds. Jesus adds, "I am going to prepare a place for you," and this also, "I am coming again and will take you along to myself." That is our best picture of heaven, to be with Jesus, and thus "at home with the Lord," conformed at last to His likeness and with the likeness of children of God feeling at home in the family of God forever.

Jesus does not say whether this "coming" will be in each case by death, or His own personal coming at the end. That we can leave to Him. The early Christians did hope that the Lord's return might be while they were alive. But Jesus had repeatedly told them that no one knew when it would be. The important thing was, and is, to be ready for His coming. But this blessed promise that He will meet us at death and take us to the Father is the Christian's joy and confident hope. With this glorious promise the believer in Christ can meet death without fear, even with exultation. So we stake all on this word of Christ.

4. Heaven then Means Being at Home with Christ and the Father and All the Redeemed.

People are often troubled for fear that they will not be able to recognize their loved ones in heaven. That is surely a groundless apprehension. On the Mount of Transfiguration, the three disciples recognized Moses and Elijah whom they had not previously seen. And here Jesus expressly says, "that where I am ye may be also." That is Christ's own picture of heaven, to be with Him. If they could not recognize Jesus, what would be the joy in being there? Saul of Tarsus "saw" Jesus on the road to Damascus. If we can recognize our Lord and Saviour, surely we can know each other. In the parable of the Rich Man and Lazarus, there is recognition on the other side. We shall all be changed and glorified beyond a doubt, but not to the destruction of personality. This picture of heaven as home gives the crowning consummation of eternal love and life. There is no idea of idleness or stagnation in this conception, but of growth in love and likeness to Christ, of worship and praise, of unending fellowship with God. In Revelation 21:1-4, the new heaven is described as a city, the holy Jerusalem coming down out of heaven from God. It is like a bride adorned for her husband. God makes His "tabernacle" with men, as in the garden of Eden before sin entered. Sin cannot enter here, nor death, nor sorrow, nor crying, nor toil. God Himself will wipe away every tear from our eyes. What a picture of glory is this! And then in Revelation 22:1-5 we see the river of the water of life flowing out of the throne of God and of the Lamb. No drought, no curse, no night, no darkness here; no darkness and no need of the light of the sun, for the Lord God is the light in this new garden of God. Beautiful imagery is this, but even so, the reality must be far beyond it all.

5. And Jesus is Our Guide to Our Home.

Jesus said, "And where I am going, ye know the way." He has not left us alone in the wilderness to find the way to our heavenly home. That statement to the apostles describes all the previous teaching of Christ. But it disturbed Thomas, who had a sceptical turn of mind, and held clearly a materialistic conception of heaven, for he took up this remark of Jesus and said: "Lord, we do not know where you are going; how do we know the way?" Peter had asked, "Where are you going?" But Jesus had not answered except in His symbolic language about the Father's house, which Thomas did not comprehend. Thomas is a fair representative of the blighting doubt which has induced so many to look on themselves as mere animals with no immortality before them. How can Jesus answer the doubt of Thomas? He answers it in terms of personality with words as profound as any ever uttered even by the Master: "I am the way, and the truth, and the life." Jesus is the way, and the only way to the Father: "No one comes to the Father except by me." Let those words stand as the claim of Christ. They have to be faced by Confucionists, Buddhists, Jews, Mohammedans, Unitarians, Christian Scientists, Bolshevists, atheists, humanists, faddists, who follow any other false light. Call this narrow, illiberal, anything you will. There is no other way to the Father but by the Son. This is not merely John's report of Jesus. It is in substance in Q (the Logia of Jesus), in Mark's Gospel, in Matthew's Gospel, in Luke's Gospel, in Acts, in the Epistles of Paul, in Peter's Epistles, in Hebrews, in James, in Jude, in the Epistles of John, in the Apocalypse of John. Jesus is the truth about God. "He that has seen me has seen the Father." He is the life, and He alone can give life to those dead in trespasses and sins.

So then let us not complain that there are not other ways to heaven. Let us rejoice that there is this way and walk in it here and now. Paul makes it his "ambition" (II Cor. 5:9 f) to be well-pleasing to Jesus Christ, before whom we must all stand and render an account of deeds done in the body, whether good or evil. We are still in the tent of the body, but some day, please God and praise God, we shall drop this temporary abode and enter into that glorious home of the soul, prepared for us by the Lord Jesus, who will welcome us and make us feel at home through all eternity.

44.85
14.00
9.00

67.85